ULTRA SUCCESS

12 STEPS TO POWER PERFORMANCE

ULM
ULTRA LEAD

D1666460

ASHMORET MISHAL

DEDICATION

This book is dedicated to all of my mentors, coaches, and running partners, who inspired me to develop The Ultra Leadership Method™ and pass it on to others.

ACKNOWLEDGEMENTS

I want to thank my first running coach and life mentor, the person who taught me the most important lessons in life.

Eilon Beja is a special man who took me under his wing and led me to cross the finish line of my very first marathon. By training me both physically and mentally during my developing years as a teenager, he also helped me to achieve many other goals in life.

Author's Note

This book is the written version of The Ultra Leadership Method – The Coaching Technique for Setting Ultra Goals & Achieving Them, using the "12 Steps to Success" model that I created after eight years of experience coaching people and helping them to achieve their goals. You can use these steps to achieve your own personal or business goals, too, by following the tasks at the end of each chapter. I advise you to manage your personal "Goals Achievement Diary" from Step One. I invite you to visit my website: https://ultra.training and to enroll in my online courses on Udemy:

www.udemy.com/user/ashmoret-mishal

TABLE OF CONTENTS

INTRODUCTION

What is the Best Leadership Education?

"Sports are a tool for achieving one's goals and a path to self-empowerment...They incorporate setting goals and then making them happen. That's what I like about running."

- Ashmoret "Ash" Mishal

I would like to share my background and ideas about running, leadership, and psychology—together, these understandings have formed the basis for the method and achievement model that I developed to empower people's abilities to set long-term goals and achieve them, as well as to overcome challenges of sports training by using long-distance running techniques.

In October of 2016, I was interviewed by Israel's leading health and fitness magazine, *Menta*. The following excerpt from their article describes the process I went through before deciding to develop this method.

"The only way to deal with pain is to give in to it. You just say to yourself, 'Okay, now my calf muscles hurt.' Then a few minutes later, you say, 'Now it's my little finger.'

"Each time, you need to focus on a different body part or dominant limb. But you don't let it stop you.

"When giving a lecture, I tell everyone to stand on one leg and tell me when the burning sensation starts. Then I tell them to imagine that burning going on for 39 hours straight while you're running an ultramarathon. But, when you are out training or competing, you experience pain differently."

At the age of 24, Mishal was the youngest ultrarunner in Israel. She has run nine full marathons and ultramarathons of 38 miles, 60 miles and 90 miles. She was the female champion of the longest international race held in Israel, which is 125 miles long.

"I ran my first marathon when I was 19, during my military service. It was a turning point in my life—that was when I realized how much the marathon is a metaphor and a self-empowerment tool for one's life."

Mishal's experience as an ultramarathon runner, running coach and leadership trainer after her military service in the Israeli army was the basis behind her vision to develop The Ultra

Leadership Method and her 12 Steps to Success course.

"I have trained many running groups and have always been frustrated by the fact that my trainees returned home with nothing more than cramps and muscle pain. I wanted more than that for them. I wanted running to give them something extra, an additional value beyond the benefit of physical fitness...

"The ideas I implement in The Ultra Leadership Method came to me while I was running a 90-mile ultramarathon. About halfway in, I experienced a very difficult moment. After running constantly for 45 miles, my body demanded that I quit. I had to stop and lay down on the track.

"After a few minutes, I picked myself up to continue and suddenly realized—this is what leadership is all about. And just as I was picking myself up at this hard time of personal crisis, I knew that this realization could help people develop leadership skills that would be valuable for them in work and in life.

"When I had this epiphany, I realized that this is what I'd been searching for, for a very long time."

MENTORSHIP

A lot of people ask me why am I so eager to mentor others. Why do I share my knowledge with others, instead of hogging it all for myself?

Thanks to my first running coach, who later became my life mentor, I learned how amazing it is to tap into abundance and generosity, and to be able to share what you know with other people, enrich their lives, and empower them to do well and succeed.

In an interview with journalist Dina Abramson, which was published in the online Israeli magazine, The Best One, under the title "The Iron Lady—About Mentorship and Fighting Stereotypes," I discussed how I came to become a running coach:

While still in high school, I returned to Israel from Chicago with my mother and sister, and I found myself feeling very bored at school. In the US, my school schedule had been hectic and usually included extracurricular sports activities. While living in the US, I had a sense of self-fulfillment at school, so after moving back to Israel at age 16, I persuaded my family and my school to let me be excused twice a week from school so I could take a training course at the Wingate Institute, Israel's top sports training facility, and that's how I started.

When I got there, I observed that most of the guys participating in the course were around 40 years old, and were doing career retraining. They stared at me like I was some kind of rare bird, as if asking "Girl, what are you doing here?" I just stared back at them, as if asking "What are YOU doing here?" I wanted to be a trainer! People find it odd when someone knows at such a young age what they want to be when they grow up. But I'm all for it, and that's something that I teach today in the leadership courses I give to adolescents. If you find something you are passionate about, don't wait, just do it! At the same time, my mother's life partner, Eilon Beja, became my running coach and mentor, and within two years he had me running my very first marathon of 26 miles in Jerusalem.

I started running training with Eilon when I was 17, and when I was 19 he told me, "Ashmoret, in two weeks you're going to run the Jerusalem marathon and you're going to complete it." Of course, I never believed I could do it, and nobody else believed so either.

Actually, nobody thought I should even be running at all. He enrolled me and I managed to run the entire 26 miles.

I had realized a dream—it was a life-changing experience that taught me that success is possible, even in the face of belief or disbelief. It was a point in my life that contributed to an overall sense of accomplishment and capability.

It was that instant that I realized that there was something else to learn through running, which I couldn't learn anywhere else at such a young age. Running is an amazing educational tool for developing determination, resilience, perseverance, willpower, ability and awareness, as it is for promoting personal development.

Running 125 Miles

In the moments before I ran a 125-mile ultramarathon, I remember feeling very excited and nervous. The course consisted of six rounds of about 20 miles each, and included some very challenging terrain, with sections of uphill, downhill, gravel, cobblestones, sand, and dirt. I didn't really know what was going on around me. We had to run the course, which was a little harsh, again and again and again and again...

As I ran, I experienced an entire spectrum of emotions, from excitement, happiness, hope, optimism, and love, all the way to the complete opposite... despair, crisis, weakness, depression, and anger.

The most difficult part of the marathon was starting the second night of running, because there is something about that darkness, that aloneness, that gloominess, that suddenly creeps up on you and makes you feel even more exhausted and lonely. After so many hours of being awake and on my feet, I felt like I was no longer there, that something in me had ascended toward the sky, leaving only my body behind.

I saw myself in the worst condition I'd ever been in, at a profoundly deep low—in crisis.

It was quite scary, because I suddenly found myself confronting my worst fear, the fear of having great regrets. My greatest regret would have been if I'd quit without completely coping with the challenge, after doing so much, after coming so far. How could I even think of quitting? Of simply giving up?

I felt a kind of anger at myself. I found myself thinking things like, "You're such a loser," and, "How can you just give up?"

I discuss these issues in the documentary movie about me by Mika Orr, 125-Mile Ultramarathon Race:

THE ULTRA LEADERSHIP METHOD

Running is much more than a way to achieve physical fitness and do strength training. It is an excellent tool for developing personal leadership values and self-management tools—a field I was engaged in during my military service.

A great deal of research has been done on the link between achievement-based sports, such as marathon running, and success in our professional and personal lives. The 12-step program that I have created is designed to guide people of all ages down the mental and physical path that any long-distance runner takes on their way to accomplishing long-term goals, whether those goals be athletic or professional.

The methodological approach I offer includes skills and steps, where the first step is to set a goal and the final step is in achieving this same goal.

The underlying belief behind this approach is that we are not born to be successful—we train to succeed.

12 STEPS
TO
POWER
PERFORMANCE

STEP 1
SET A GOAL FOR YOUR VISION!
That is going to be your
S.M.A.R.T destination :
Specific, measurable,
attainable, realistic and timely.

STEP 2
ASSESS YOUR CURRENT
SITUATION!
That is going to be your
starting point!

STEP 3
CHOOSE A SUITABLE GOAL!
Make sure your goal is both
ideal & realistic.

STEP 4
PLAN YOUR PATH!
Lay-out the road map that
will take you from point A
To point B.

STEP 5
PICK YOUR MILESTONES!
Break down the ULTRA goal
into micro & S.M.A.R.T goals

STEP 6
BE SELF - AWARE!
Know what your strength,
weakness, opportunity
and threat are.

STEP 7
BE CHALLENGED!
Identify the challenges on the
Way to achieving your goal &
practice their solutions.

STEP 8
BE PERSISTENT!
Increase your GRIT by
Empowering your passion &
Perseverance.

STEP 9
MANAGE ANY CRISIS!
Practice and improve your
Emotional Stamina & coping
Techniques!

STEP 10
RE-ASSESS YOUR GOAL!
Gain more status control by
Adapting to possible changes!

STEP 11
SELF - CONTROL!
Before reaching a new pick
And success!

STEP 12
SUCCESS!
Enjoy your success &
Set a new meaningful goal!

WWW.ULTRALEADERSHIPMETHOD.COM

STEP 1 – SETTING A GOAL

"A journey of a thousand miles begins with a single step!"

- Lao Tzu, Chinese philosopher

A study conducted in 2007 by Dr. Gail Matthews of Dominican University in Illinois found that students who wrote down their goals or reported their progress to friends had a greater chance of achieving their goals than those who did not set any goals, report their progress to friends, or write down their goals. By writing down their goals or sharing them with friends, these students created accountability. The study found that the level of commitment students had in achieving their goals was higher among those who had written down their goals, and that because their level of commitment in achieving their goals was higher, their drive was therefore stronger.

Setting a goal is the first step on the path to success. Identifying your goal is a significant step because we first need to know what we want to achieve. The Dominican University study shows that goal setting is often not taken as seriously as it needs to be if you want to succeed. It also demonstrates that it is impossible to skip this step if we seek to achieve our goals.

There are three types of goals in our program. The first type of goal, and the longest-term one, is your ultra-goal. This is your long-term goal that you want to achieve in three to five years. The second type of goal is your mid-term goal. This is a goal that you hope to achieve in about one year. The third and final type of goal is your short-term goal. This is a goal you can successfully complete in about three months from your starting point.

It is important to keep in mind that all of these goals should directly relate to each other. Your short-term goal should lead you to achieve the mid-term goal, and your mid-term goal should lead you on the way to achieving your ultra-goal.

However, choosing a goal is alone not enough: We have to set smart and effective goals in order to increase the chance of achieving them.

The SMART Model

SMART is an acronym for a model that describes a method for setting effective goals. By following these five parameters for goal setting, you can set yourself up for success. SMART stands for:

S   Specificity

M   Measurability

A   Attainability

R   Realistic Expectations

T   Timeframe

Example

When we choose a goal in sports, it is easy to identify its characteristics in terms of specificity, measurability, and usually, attainability. A sports goal is measurable. For example, the goal of running five miles has a numeric value and can be easily measured by distance. You know that if you only run four miles, you have not succeeded. But as soon as you hit five miles, you have.

By adding a deadline by which we hope to achieve our goal, we also fulfill the definition of our timeframe.

Later on, in the steps that follow, we will discuss how to determine if the goal we have set is realistic.

Before we go on, it is important to distinguish between a vision and a goal. A vision is a final goal that consists of smaller goals. Unlike SMART model goals, a vision is more general; it is somewhat obscure or vague, like a dream. This isn't to say that we shouldn't have a vision. On the contrary, it is important that we do, because thinking about our vision takes us through a meaningful process as it guides us in pursuit of our related, smaller-scale goals.

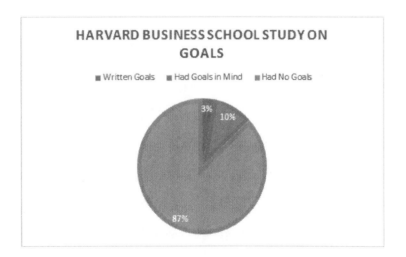

Golden Circle

In his book and TED Talk lecture, motivational speaker and leadership researcher Simon Sinek illustrates the main qualities that distinguish successful leaders from others. He observes that the fact that successful leaders have a why—a true purpose and deeper reason for their actions. Successful leaders have a greater vision of the direction in which they want to lead their companies. By contrast, those who attempt to make a major social or business change while lacking the focus and belief in a greater vision (a *why*), are significantly less successful.

Sinek refers to his model as the Golden Circle, where the outer layer represents the *what*, the middle layer represents the *how*, and the inner layer, the core, represents the *why*. The first question anyone who wants to succeed should ask themselves is *why*. Answering this question—identifying and naming the why—often takes a great deal of time, effort, and reflection.

Identifying our original motive and keeping it constantly in mind is important throughout the entire process of achieving our goals. At many times along the endless and challenging path to success, we may start to doubt ourselves and ask, "What am I doing here?" or "Why am I doing this to myself?" Asking ourselves these kinds of *why* questions helps us to clarify our greater purpose. But knowing the *why* behind our endeavors will keep us motivated on our path to success.

There are three main types of challenges and questions arise during the pursuit of "ultra" goals:

1. What are you going to do when everyone around you is telling you to quit?
2. What are you going to do when even you don't know if you can make it?
3. What are you going to do when you are out of resources?

Take a few moments to think about these questions and to answer them.

Having a greater motive and sense of mission will help you overcome these social, internal and materialistic challenges.

G O A L   S E T T I N G
T A S K

Step 1 – Task

1. Define and write down your vision.

2. Decide what your long, mid and short tem
    S.M.A.R.T goals are (specificity, measurability,
    attainability, realistic expectations, and
    timeframe).

YOUR
EXERCISES
OUTDOOR

STEP 1 – SETTING A GOAL: OUTDOOR EXERCISES

When we set our goal, it's important to recall the Golden Circle (What, How, Why) and to strongly emphasize the meaningful purpose and reason for the goal we decide to set.

When we talk about "why" we choose a certain goal, we talk about a greater vision or a dream, and it is this vision that inspires us to take an action!

❖ Every time I go outside for a run or an outdoor workout, I become very inspired and motivated. When I exercise outside, watching the changing views and people around me, I am able to clear my mind and release my thoughts. Outdoor training for me is the best time to relax, and to become more creative.

❖ Here is the fitness section of my outdoor exercises that I encourage you to practice, at the level of your ability, so that as you become inspired, you are also able to improve your physical shape!

❖ **Disclaimer:** Consult with your physician or other health care professional before starting this or any other fitness program to determine if it is right for your needs. Do not start this fitness program if your physician or health care provider advises against it. If you experience faintness, dizziness, pain or shortness of breath at any time while exercising, you should stop immediately.

LEGS PULL-UP

Set/Time: Hold pose for 5-10 seconds

1. Lie against a wall or a pole and lift your legs straight until they reach the line of your hips or above. Hold position for at least 10 seconds.

2. Inhale as you uncurl back to the start position, going slowly to protect your back.

AIR CRUNCH

Set/Time: Hold pose for 10-15 seconds

1. Lie against a wall or a pole and lift your bent legs until they reach the line of your hips or above. Hold position for at least 10 seconds.
2. Inhale as you uncurl back to the start position, going slowly to protect your back.

WARRIOR

Set/Time: Hold pose 15-30 seconds (each side)

1. Hug your left shin into your chest, and then extend it straight back behind you so it's parallel to the ground.
2. Reach your arms out in front of you so your body is in a straight line from your fingertips on, with a slight shoulder and hip twist.

STRAIGHT LEGS PUSH-UP

Set/Time: Hold pose 5-10 seconds

1. Sit down with your legs straight in front of you. Put your hands behind you and across from your hips.

2. Take a big breath, tighten your abs, and lift your body with your straight legs so your knees are about 4-6 inches from the floor.

DEEP PUSH-UP

Set/Time: Hold pose 15-30 seconds

1. Stand tall, hold bars with your feet wide apart.

2. Slowly bend your arms with your elbows at 90 degree angles. Breathe deeply and slowly return to the start position, and perform the exercise another 10 to 15 times.

PUSH UP

Set/Time: 10-15 repetitions

1. With your arms straight and slightly wider than shoulder width apart, stand with your feet perpendicular to the floor.

2. Slowly bend your arms with your elbows at 90 degree angles. Breathe deeply and slowly return to the start position, and perform the exercise another 10 to 15 times.

ARM BEND

Set/Time: Hold pose 10-15 repetitions (each side)

1. Stand with your feet perpendicular to the bench and with your right arm straight on the bench, supporting your body weight.

2. Slowly bend your right arm with your elbows in almost 90 degree angles. Breathe deeply and slowly return to the start position, and perform the exercise another 10 to 15 times.

CHEST EXTENSION

Set/Time: Hold pose 15-30 seconds

1. Stand tall, draw your abs in, and pull your shoulders backward with your elbows straight.
2. Lean forward with your chest, and keep your body straight and strong with your feet in line under your hands.

STEP 2 – SITUATION ASSESSMENT

"It is good to have an end to journey toward: but it is the journey that matters, in the end."

-Ursula K. Le Guin

Laura Gentile, Senior Vice President of espnW and Women's Initiatives at ESPN, gave insight on 'how playing a sport can get women to the C-suite':

"The more women play sports, the more likely their skills will transcend into the professional world. At espnW, we have completed two studies with our partner EY that prove the connection between competing in athletics and success in the workforce. We've uncovered various data that illustrates female athletes make great leaders. In a survey of 400 women executives, 52% of C-suite women played sport at the university level, compared to 39% of women at other management levels. The correlation between success on the playing field and success in the workplace is indisputable. Girls who play sports have greater social and economic mobility, grow up healthy and confident, and perform better in school. In fact, 74% of executive women agreed that a background in sports can help accelerate a woman's leadership and career potential."

This study and many others on the subject illustrate the link between success in achievement-based sports and success in business careers. I noticed this pattern myself six years ago, when I ran my first marathon. Many of my marathon mates and other runners participating in that marathon event in Israel were commanders and officers in the security forces, businesspersons, and executives.

Using a roadmap as a metaphor, I will demonstrate how the physical course that my runners follow while training with me, and that I, too, go through during long-distance training and competing, is similar in many aspects to the path toward long-term goals in life or business.

Creating a Cognitive Roadmap

To illustrate the first four steps to success, think about the modus operandi used by a map app, such as Google Maps. First, we enter "Where To"—our destination. Next, we enter "Where From"—our current location. Finally, we click "Calculating Route" and we receive an outlined plan for overcoming the gap between our starting point and our finish point. Now, let's take running a marathon as an example.

A person who runs five miles every day signs up to participate in a marathon competition. His goal is to run 26.2 miles, but he can currently run only 5 miles. This means that he must make a training plan or an action plan to take him along the best route to achieving his goal.

Understanding the starting point is as important as understanding the final point that we want to reach. In running, it is simple—we assess our condition by performing a fitness or running test. But understanding the starting point and end point in business situations can be more challenging. It is important that you compare apples to apples in order to develop a fair assessment of your business situation. For instance, if you have chosen a monetary goal of revenue in dollars, you should assess your current revenue in dollars as well, and not in terms of units sold or number of customers.

Evaluating our condition helps us to set realistic expectations with the very first step, where we use the SMART model. Is our goal realistic? This step of assessing our situation leads us to build an action plan that contains the necessary steps we need to take in order to reach our goal.

Finally, if we conclude that our goal is not realistic because of its timeframe or measurement, based on our current situation assessment, we then reset our original goal and adapt it to our current ability. It is essential to be flexible to changes and perform adjustments if necessary.

SWOT Model

SWOT is an acronym that helps us assess our situations when determining our personal or business goal, and it includes four aspects:

S Strength

W Weakness

O Opportunity

T Threat

The SWOT model is used in the business and organizational world as a tool for evaluating our situation prior to making a decision. It includes two internal dimensions, strengths and weaknesses, and two external dimensions, opportunities and threats.

The SWOT model can be applied to your business goals as well as fitness goals, but it should not be applied to you on a personal level as a businessperson. It is extremely important to consider the components that have both direct or indirect effects on your goals and to take them into consideration when setting your goals. Always be focused on your end goal, what you are trying to achieve in your ultimate vision, and what you can do to make them happen – or not happen! Look honestly at your strengths, weaknesses, opportunities, and threats to assess your situation and determine where you want to go.

The SWOT model takes positive and negative values into account. The positive values are strengths and opportunities, and the negative values are threats and weaknesses, and they should all be taken into consideration in order to make a responsible and calculated decision.

These four aspects came into play while I was preparing to run my first ultramarathon race of 60 miles. Before that, I had run only five full marathons, and I had just six months to train for the 60-mile race. My plan, as my coach Eilon Beja shared with me, was to run a marathon each week. And so, for about four months, I ran almost a full marathon on a weekly basis. But one day, six weeks before the race, I suffered from a serious sports injury to my knee, and developed iliotibial band syndrome (ITBS).

At that point, I realized that there were only a few women registered for the race, and there were only four women participating in my age category, females under 40. My threat was obviously my severe sports injury.

My chances of standing on the podium as a winner seemed unlikely at that point. My weakness was that I was accustomed to running at a relatively fast speed. That was the way I had been trained. It took a long time for me to break that habit and to begin running at a moderate pace that was more suitable for long distances. I also lacked the necessary physical strength: My strength was derived mainly from my mental resolution to cross the finishing line.

Rethinking these circumstances, I decided to take a break from running and receive physiotherapy. I didn't want to risk a worse injury and greater pain. Eventually, I decided to compete anyway—just not with the aim of winning or of achieving a competitive time.

After 14:40 hours, I crossed the 60-mile race finish line. I came in after Limor Bigon but before Dganit Kuplik, winning second place in my category.

Social Comparison

Many of the choices we make are based on our current

assessment and evaluation. The reason why Step 1 –

"Setting a Goal" is prior to Step 2 – "Assessing the

Situation," is because we first want to aspire high and

think BIG, without too many distractions and mind-

limitations. But very often, when we then realize that our

point B (destination) is extremely far away from point A

(location), we can become less motivated. Especially if we

compare ourselves to others that have already achieved

the "ultra" success we are aiming to. Some people tend to

compete with others, and prefer to be the "last among the best", and others prefer to be the "first among the mediocre". In any case, the Ultra Leadership Method approach is "challenge by choice", meaning – we believe every participant is there to compete with themselves.

When we fail to focus on our own condition and personal goals, our performance may be decreased.

SITUATION
ASSESSMENT
TASK

Step 2 – Task

1. Write down your current S.M.A.R.T assessment.

2. Explain what is your S.W.O.T assessment.

YOUR
EXERCISES
ARMS

STEP 2 – SITUATION ASSESSMENT: ARMS EXERCISE

When setting a goal, it's important to be inspired, to be motivated, and to have in mind a great reason to achieve your goal. And in addition, it's essential that you have the right mindset, skills, tools, resources, and aid.

❖ For a long time, I thought that running long distances well was a matter of having strong legs. But, when I started my first ultramarathon race (60 miles), I began to understand that when the legs become extremely tired after a few hours, the main contributing factor to successfully finish the race is the upper body – especially the arms, as the arms push you forward and aid you in your more difficult moments.

❖ Situation assessment is your guide that will lead you toward your goal. Just as working with my arms as a tool to help me with finish my race, assessing your ability and shape is a tool that will help you to set the right goal and to be in control of your work and progress.

❖ Here is the fitness section of my arms and shoulders exercises that I encourage you to practice, at the level of your ability, so that you become more inspired, as well as improve your physical shape!

- ❖ **Disclaimer**: Consult with your physician or other health care professional before starting this or any other fitness program to determine if it is right for your needs. Do not start this fitness program if your physician or health care provider advises against it. If you experience faintness, dizziness, pain or shortness of breath at any time while exercising you should stop immediately.

STATIC WIDE PUSH-UP

Set/Time: Hold pose 10-20 seconds

1. Place your two hands bent comfortably wide apart on a bench.

2. Keeping your abs tight, and your posture straight without an arch, breathe deeply as you hold the position.

STATIC NARROW PUSH-UP

Set/Time: Hold pose 10-20 seconds

1. Place your hands close together and bent on a bench.

2. Keeping your abs tight, and your posture straight without an arch, breathe deeply as you hold the position.

Ashmoret Mishal   Ultra Success | 54

DYNAMIC PUSH-UP

Set/Time: 10-20 repetitions

1. On a low bench, with your arms straight and slightly wider than shoulder width apart, support your body on your hands and toes.
2. Inhale as you bend your arms and lower your upper body until your chest is about 4-6 inches away from the bench.

ARMS TWIST

Set/Time: 10-20 repetitions (each side)

1. Place one hand on the end of a low bench and the other hand straight in line with your ear. Keep your neck long and your chin tucked in.
2. Inhale and hold your body steady as you switch and alternate hands to the other side.

SIDE DYNAMIC PUSH-UP

Set/Time: 10-20 repetitions (each side)

1. Place your right hand straight on the end of a low bench, with your body held at a diagonal to the side, and your right foot grounded to the floor.

2. Inhale as you bend your right arm and lower your upper body by bending your arm 2-4 inches.

SIDE STATIC PUSH-UP

Set/Time: 10-20 repetitions (each side)

1. Place your right hand straight on the end of a low bench, with your body held at a diagonal to the side, and your right foot grounded to the floor.

2. Keeping your abs tight, and your posture straight without an arch, breathe deeply as you hold position.

BACK ARMS EXTENSION

Set/Time: 10-20 repetitions (each side)

1. Stand straight with your left arm behind your back, holding a sleeve or a resistance band, with a 90-degree angle. Hold the end of the band with your right hand extended.

2. Keeping your abs tight, exhale as you bend your right arm backward and down towards your left hand, and then extend it back to the original position.

ARMS EXTENSION

Set/Time: 10-20 repetitions

1. Sit with your back straight and your arms extended to the sides, holding sleeves or a resistance band.

2. Keeping your abs tight, exhale as you slightly bend your arms and then extend them to the starting position.

STEP 3 – CHOOSING A SUITABLE GOAL

"The greater danger for most of us is not that our aim is too high and we miss it, but that it is too low and we hit it."

-Michelangelo di Lodovico Buonarroti Simoni

In May of 2016, the magazine *Runner's World* published a special issue about the Boston Marathon, one of the oldest annual marathons in the world. Starring in the article was Bobby (Roberta) Gibb, who made American history as the first female marathon runner in the U.S. in 1966.

When Gibb signed up for the marathon, she received a letter in her mailbox from the Amateur Athletic Association (AAU) stating that women were physiologically unable to run a marathon distance, and that under the rules of the AAU, women were not allowed to run more than a mile in a competitive running race.

While that may sound puzzling and irrational for Millennials, at that time it was accepted as common knowledge that women were not capable of competing in a race any longer than a single mile, and nor should they be allowed to. That was when Gibb realized that in addition to her personal will to run a marathon, she also had a greater social cause, a vision. It became much more important to her to attend the marathon and cross that finish line because of the social significance it carried.

"It was a crucial moment in the development of social consciousness. It had changed the way men think about women, and it changed the way women think about themselves. It replaced the false belief in a new reality. How can you prove you can do something, if you're not allowed to do it? If we could have done something that seems impossible, what else can women do? What else can people accomplish that is perceived as impossible?"

-Bobbi Gibb

Bobbi Gibb | Photograph by Jeff Johnson

Five decades after Gibb and other female marathon-running pioneers came along, these including such athletes as Katherine Switzer, gender statistics in long distance running events in the U.S. have completely transformed. As of 2010, the percentage of women participants in running events has almost equaled that of men. In the Boston Marathon of 2015, about 45 percent of the participants were women. The inspirational story of the pioneer Bobbi Gibb illustrates the importance of accumulating experiences in order to better evaluate ourselves.

Hopping Exercise

One of the leadership exercises that I give my mentees involves having them hop on one foot for thirty consecutive seconds. Before they do so, I ask them to roughly estimate the maximum number of hops they can perform during that given timeframe. Before I share the results of this exercise, **please don't read any further** before conducting this simulation exercise for yourself.

Document both your initial estimate and your result.

My estimation is: _____

My result is: _____

People generally underestimate themselves, and this often becomes evident in this exercise. Most participants believe that they can only perform 20 to 30 hops. Yet, to their surprise, they usually hop three to five times more than their initial estimation would suggest. One reason for this common misassumption is that the participants have never performed this exercise before, so of course they are going to assess themselves inaccurately. Yet, why does this lead them to under-evaluate instead of over-evaluate their ability?

We have a natural tendency to underestimate our abilities and potential, and we are inclined to be afraid of taking risks, experimenting, or betting or gambling. We fear feelings of disappointment and regret. It is much easier to be surprised for the better by getting higher results than we anticipated, rather than to experience failure in our performance—at least, that's the assumption. However, this kind of mindful shielding is very likely to generate a lack of confidence in the long run—if we continue to avoid taking any risks or continue to under-evaluate our abilities.

In other words, if we do not try, we do not accurately know what we are worth. It is important to dare! As Michelangelo said, "The biggest mistake is not to aim high and miss, but to aim low and hit."

Ideal Realistic Goals

If the process of reaching a goal appears too difficult in relation to its desired value, people are prone to giving up. To keep your motivation high, you need to find the right level of challenge, one that is not too easy, but not too challenging that it feels impossible. One source of motivation that helps keep people motivated to reach a goal is the confidence that the goal is achievable. Moreover, when people see and control their progress toward their goal and can identify the end of that process, their level of certainty and commitment to the process increases.

When people train in any form of sports, they generally receive immediate feedback for their work, as well as attain a suitable outcome for their efforts. For example, a person who is out of shape and suddenly starts to train in running will notice a fast and immediate improvement in their progress, as well as an improvement in their training. This usually happens after a short period of training. For example, a person who can run one mile manages to run two miles, and then three, four, and so on. Each time they train, there is a noticeable improvement in the distance they can run, the speed at which they do it, and the stamina they sustain.

Though setting goals for business success may not have the physical and visible immediate feedback of athletic goals, it is possible to set goals that allow for clear and identifiable feedback. If you have established a goal following the SMART guidelines, this will help ensure that you are able to receive the necessary feedback to see if you are on track to achieve your goals.

When we receive immediate feedback, especially when we make a positive improvement, our sense of motivation and desire to achieve our goal skyrockets. Getting feedback and staying motivated throughout our journey towards success is very important to increase the chances of long-term goal achievement.

There are three main types of goals, ranging from beginner to advanced. The first type of goal is the "realistic goal" – this is one that we are confident we can achieve, as it often does not even require us working at our full potential. This is a good goal for new athletes or entrepreneurs who are just beginning their endeavors or are exploring new areas of expertise.

The second type of goal is an "ideal goal." This type of goal is more challenging and requires a greater level of our effort and abilities. An ideal goal will put you on track to reach 100% of your potential, and is suitable for intermediate athletes and entrepreneurs.

The third and final type of goal is a "stretched goal." This is an expanded goal that goes beyond our full potential, and if we look honestly at our current situation, we cannot be certain that we will definitely achieve this goal.

Stretched Goals

Stretched goals are intended to be challenging—goals beyond the individual's current performance level. This type of goal requires individuals to push themselves beyond their limits, through tremendous effort and endeavors. One should keep in mind that a stretched goal typically goes far beyond a person's actual potential. Thus, even without achieving 100% of a stretched goal, the individual's ability would still extend beyond their previous limitations. This type of goal is ideal for athletes and entrepreneurs who are risk-takers or are very experienced.

Long Term Planning

Long-term planning is a more complicated task than many realize, in which we are required to do some higher level thinking unless we are more experienced in the relevant kinds of tasks.

On the first step of the 12 Steps to Success model, we noticed that we perform better when we are committed to achieving certain goals, which emphasizes the importance of strategic goal setting. Setting the right goal is nonetheless a critical skill: we must learn how to effectively set goals. The main message that we take out of this training session on Step 3 is the setting of the right goal, which should be both ideal and realistic.

If we set a goal that is too hard for us, we may become discouraged if it appears we will not achieve it. So, we must be aware of overestimation: when our estimation turns out to be incorrect by exceeding the actual result. This refers to the common mistake of setting unrealistic goals. It is essential to know how to dream big, but also to be down-to-earth. So, whatever goal you decide upon, ensure that it is realistic and that you can achieve it in the timeframe that you set for yourself.

This goes hand in hand with the opposite problem, underestimation: when our estimation falls short of the actual result. This is another common mistake of underestimating the completion time. If we don't estimate our goal completion time properly, it can be discouraging, and sometimes even lead us to give up.

According to Burton et al. (2001), the two most critical steps in the goal implementation process are developing systematic action plans and evaluating goals regularly. Goal evaluation is considered a critical goal implementation step because it provides information about competence when performance reaches or exceeds a goal, and thus, it helps with raising self confidence and motivation. (Burton et al., 2001; Locke & Latham, 1990, 2006).

Nevertheless, an important tool for success is having the ability to **reset our goals**. As entrepreneurs and athletes, it is essential for our success that we practice being flexible to changes as they arise. Unexpected things happen, things that we could not have anticipated in our initial long-term planning, but we should not let unexpected events throw us off track.

There are two primary ways to reset goals: you can reset the measurable value (ex. Changing your goal of running 10 miles to 8 miles), or you can change the time frame (ex. Changing your goal of 3 months to 4 months). I do not recommend extending your time frame significantly, as time is key factor in your goal, and continuously postponing a goal's timeline can become an excuse for not getting things done!

Research has also shown that an effective way to learn how to set the right goal is by taking opportunities for self-evaluation and reflection, and getting specific feedback in the "goal setting" process.

S U I T A B L E
T A R G E T
T A S K

Step 3 – Task

1. Identify the types of goals you chose and explain why they are realistic / ideal / stretched.

2. According to your new assessment, do you need to reset your goals? If yes – why and how?

YOUR
EXERCISES
STRETCHING

Step 3 – Suitable Target: Stretching Exercise

A goal that we set can be under our actual ability, over our potential, or exactly right and suiting our ability.

To better accurately understand what our potential truly is, it is important to challenge ourselves and gain experience.

Here are some essential points to consider when reviewing our goals:

❖ If the goal we chose turned out to be neither ideal nor realistic, it's essential to have the quality of flexibility.

❖ Stretched goals are also a technique of setting higher targets to fulfill your potential and to gain a greater success than we thought we could achieve.

❖ The following fitness section consists of my stretching exercises that I encourage you to practice, at the level of your ability, so you improve your changes' flexibility & better stretch your goals, as well as improve your physical shape!

❖ **Disclaimer**: Consult with your physician or other health care professional before starting this or any other fitness program to determine if it is right for your needs. Do not start this fitness program if your physician or health care provider advises against it. If you experience faintness, dizziness, pain or shortness of breath at any time while exercising you should stop immediately.

STANDING PALM PRESS

Set/Time: hold pose for 15 seconds (each side)

1. Sit down with your back straight and your arms extended to the sides, holding sleeves or a resistance band.

2. Keeping your abs tight, exhale as you slightly bend your arms and then extend them to the starting position.

STANDING SIDE OPENER

Set/Time: hold pose for 15 seconds (each side)

1. Stand with your feet parallel to each other, right shoulder aligned with your hips. Inhale and reach your right arm up and over. Grab your hip with your left hand.

2. Let your torso naturally arch over to your left side. Stay here for 15 seconds and then work on the other side.

SHOULDER STRETCH

Set/Time: hold pose for 15 seconds (each side)

1. Bend your knees and fold your legs toward you as if you were coming into a seated meditation, with one foot above and one foot under the crossed ankle.
2. Put one arm across the body at shoulder height and hold it in place using the crook of your other elbow. Gently pull the straight arm toward you.

TRICEPS STRETCH

Set/Time: hold pose for 15 seconds (each

side)

1. Bend your knees and fold your legs toward you as if you were coming into a seated meditation, with one foot above and one foot under the crossed ankle.
2. Bend one arm and put it behind your head. Using the other hand, hold the hand in the back, gently assisting the stretch down. Keep the chest lifted and repeat on the other side.

NECK STRETCH

Set/Time: hold pose for 15 seconds (each side)

1. Stand tall and lift your chest, and drop your shoulders down away from your ears.
2. Gently lower your head to one side (ear to shoulder). Repeat on the opposite side.

SEATED, BOTH LEGS STRAIGHT FORWARD

Set/Time: hold pose for 15 seconds (each side)

1. Sit up tall and bring both legs straight out in front of you. Inhale and lift your left elbow backward and up.

2. As you exhale, lengthen your torso forward. If you can't easily reach your toes, slightly bend your knees.

SEATED SPINE TWIST

Set/Time: hold pose for 15 seconds (each side)

1. Sit upright. Hug your right knee to your chest and place your right foot on the ground, across and outside of your left leg so your knee is pointing straight up.
2. Exhale as you tighten your knee with your left arm closer to your chest.

HAMSTRING STRETCH

Set/Time: hold pose for 15 seconds (each side)

1. Stand tall and gently hug your right knee into your chest. Extend your right leg up and put your foot on a high surface to deepen the stretch.
2. Allow your breath to release the tension and lean towards the leg, trying to grab the right foot with your hands.

STEP 4 – BUILDING A PLAN

"World class performance comes from striving for a target just out of reach, but with a vivid awareness of how the gap might be breached. Over time, through constant repetition and deep concentration the gap will disappear, only for a new target to be created, just out of reach once again."

-Matthew Syed

If you've ever looked at a training program for marathon preparation, you were probably very surprised. The training plans are full of small details and meticulous instructions regarding various components and aspects for each day, week, and month moving toward the marathon. Usually, the training plan starts six to nine months before the competition day. Details such as distance, time, speed, pace, breaks, intervals, sets, rest, exercises, and more are filled out in training charts with definite calculated numbers.

Marathon training entails levels of discipline similar to those which successful entrepreneurs bring to their businesses. Running a marathon is not something that you can do without the proper training, just as leading a successful business does not happen without training.

Following such a training program for weeks and months on a daily basis, with great persistence and effort towards a single event that lasts for only a few hours, and does not come with any special reward upon completion, prepares long distance runners to accomplish their business tasks. Business tasks can vary from short-term to long-term tasks and plans.

This view emphasizes the importance of a well thought-out plan. Building a plan is one of the most important steps on the way to success, and we want to invest our time and work in creating a plan that will take us to the place we want to get to.

As in the example from Step 2 (Situation Assessment) regarding Google Maps, calculating the various routes available to you to reach a destination is important. You have several choices before you that differ in their efficiency. For example, choosing between the shorter route or the longer route, the faster route or the slower route.

Similarly, let us examine the 80/20 rule for efficient performance and planning:

The 80/20 rule, also known as the Pareto Principle, was suggested by management thinker Joseph M. Juran. It was named after the Italian economist Vilfredo Pareto, who observed that 80% of income in Italy was received by 20% of the Italian population. The resulting assumption is that most of the results in any situation are determined by a small number of causes. In business, the rule is used to help managers identify and determine which operating factors are the most important and should receive the most attention, based on an efficient use of resources.

The same principle applies to the idea that, if we put enough amount of time into the right planning, we can anticipate better results and outcomes. Think about time dedicated to planning as a worthwhile investment towards future performance. A plan is aimed at developing the foundation and framework of our work.

An action plan is simple, basic, and logical. It incorporates the necessary 3-5 steps that we should take in order to achieve our goal. These steps should be in a prioritized and chronological order, starting with the first and most important thing we need to do, all the way down to the last step we need to do in order to complete our goal. It is essential to focus on the steps that will lead you to achieve your goals, not just the end goal by itself.

Action plans should address the following elements:

1. Goal (where we want to go)
2. Current situation (where we are starting)
3. Resources (what we already have)
4. Constraints (what limits us)

The purpose of an action plan is to clarify what resources are required to reach the goal, formulate a timeline for when specific tasks need to be completed, and determine what resources are required. An action plan should answer the following three questions: Where am I now? (Step 2) Where do I want to go? (Step 1) What steps will I take to get there? (Step 4)

Running a business is oftentimes similar to running a marathon. As described earlier, both aspects require a good amount of planning: strategic, operational and contingent wise. Read my following interview with my marathoner friend and CEO, Ofer Sela, about his personal view on running a business and running a marathon:

> "There is a connection and a correlation between the world of running and the management of a company or a project. Every time we embark on a project, we can regard it as going for a run, a long or a short one, as the beginning of the project. Whether it is a short-term project or a long-term one, never can a project be launched without preparation and

presetting in advance. And if we make the comparison to the world of running, we will not start on the track before we know for how long, or what distance we are going to run, 5 miles, 10 miles, half a marathon? An entire marathon? How fit and ready are we to take on any specific distance?

"As in a project, to go out we need to test our equipment, such as, Is our clothing suitable for the weather? Do we need to 'fuel' ourselves with water or gels along the route? Just like any manager in charge of preparations to start a project. When we set out to run for a few hours, the runner is required to perform proper management and distribution of resources, as to not be exhausted, or 'hit the wall' (experience sudden loss of energy through athletic activities). It is necessary to run at the right pace, adequate to the distance, to drink and get energized at the proper time, so you do not get in a situation of overload on the systems of the body. During the run, we need to be wary of any external threats, like cars, dogs, rocks along the way and injuries (SWOT, anyone?).

"The runner also needs to know how to cope with crises that occur during the run, and therefore should have an alternative plan in advance, in case of any debilitating situation, like pulling a muscle or getting a sprain, for example, just as we are in the start or endpoints. If we have prepared ourselves correctly and have a mobile phone at our disposal, we can ask for help; otherwise, we might get stuck. A long run is characterized by a long time for the runner to spend with himself and his thoughts. I myself prefer to do workouts not within a group or a gathering of runners, but rather run solo, attentive to my body and leaving the head to be clear for contemplation.

"For me, a long run is an excellent time to meditate and find solutions to problems and questions if I faced them at work or in other aspects of my life. I usually tend to come up with an issue and examine it from several managerial among other aspects, looking for deeper meanings in relation to the surrounding peripheral systems. Always at the end of a run, it is a necessity to check that everything is intact and in place, do your stretching exercises, and relieve pressure and tension, preparing all the gear for the next run or project. It is also important to keep a proper diet, in order to restore what the body has consumed during the exercise, and to know when to take a break for recovery..."

Contingency Plan

The contingency plan (also known as your Plan B!) is also an important plan to develop, as often reality does not match the planning that we've done on paper. A contingency plan is a back-up plan that ensures our chances to achieve the goals, just in a different way than we had originally expected. When thinking about your contingency plan, it is helpful to think outside the box.

Contingency plans need to be more creative, as you need to think about the different variables that could come into play as you work towards your goal.

Let us go back again to the Google Maps example—once we set the destination and location, it calculates the paths, which vary in distance and time. Some of the routes are longer but faster, some are shorter but more expensive, etc. These are different plans that are made to overcome the gap between the starting point and the end point.

Different plan options should be taken into consideration when we think about where we want to go, and so we must be open-minded to different options, strategies, and tactics, as well be open to creative thinking and flexibility in making changes.

Do not get confused or discouraged by the idea of a contingency plan. It does not mean that you are picking a different goal and abandoning your initial one; rather, it means that you are picking a different strategy to help you achieve your goal in case your original plan fails. Though it is never pleasant to think about roadblocks or failures, it is important to be ready for these scenarios in advance so that you do not get thrown off course.

If you are working with a team towards your goal, brainstorming as a group is an effective and efficient way to come up with new ideas and strategies to deal with possible changes to the overall plan.

MAKING A PLAN
TASK

Step 4 – Task

1. Design an action plan that incorporates the necessary steps to achieve your goal, taking into consideration your resources and limitations.

2. Write down your contingency plan.

You can view a YouTube presentation of these ideas here:

YOUR
EXERCISES
ABS

STEP 4 – PLANNING: ABS EXERCISES

Goal setting is an essential factor on our path to success in both physical and professional goals. Stamina, crisis management, and persistence are powerful qualities of successful people, and are also the main keys to success. Yet, these qualities alone are not all you need, and surely not enough. To achieve your goal, you also need a plan, and a good one!

❖ The plan is your guide and a type of "bible" – describing what you should do or not do, the action steps you need to take, the milestones, and the strategies, tactics, and rules.

❖ A great comparison to emphasize the importance of the planning step is to think of using our "core muscles" as a metaphor for our plan. The core muscles function as stabilizers, and are also responsible for most full-body functional movement. Like your core muscles to your body, your plan is the core of our goal and moves us toward succeeding in it.

❖ Here is the fitness section of my core exercises that I encourage you to practice, at the level of your ability, so you can improve your goals' core, as well as improve your physical shape!

- ❖ **Disclaimer**: Consult with your physician or other health care professional before starting this or any other fitness program to determine if it is right for your needs. Do not start this fitness program if your physician or health care provider advises against it. If you experience faintness, dizziness, pain or shortness of breath at any time while exercising you should stop immediately.

SIT UP

Set/Time: 20-40 repetitions

1. Lie down and bend your knees. Place your hands beside you and behind your head, keeping your elbows out straight.

2. Keeping your abs tight, exhale as you roll up to a straightened position. Keep your chin high and look forward.

STATIC CRUNCH

Set/Time: hold pose for 30-60 seconds

1. Sit and hold your knees bent in the air. Place your hands beside you and in front of you, palms in, keeping your elbows out straight.

2. Keeping your abs tight, exhale as you hold the crunch pose with your legs bent above the ground. Keep your chin high and look forward.

STRAIGHT CRUNCH

Set/Time: hold pose for 15-30 seconds

1. Lie back with your elbow and palms on the ground, supporting your posture.
2. Keeping your abs tight, exhale as you hold your legs up straight out from your chest.

HALF PIKE

Set/Time: hold pose for 10-20 repetitions

1. Hold in a crunch posture with your legs straight above the surface. Place your hands straight behind your head, palms up.

2. Keeping your abs tight, exhale as you roll up to a static crunch. Keeping your chin high and hold in the posture for 5-10 seconds.

SIDE PLANK

Set/Time: hold pose for 15-30 seconds

1. Lie on your side and raise yourself up on one elbow, with one palm flat on the ground, and keep your feet perpendicular to the floor.

2. Hold your hip in the air, away from the surface. Extend your other arm straight up in line with your ear and open your chest.

PLANK

Set/Time: hold pose for 30-60 seconds

1. Start in a push-up position. Place your hands flat on the surface, elbows directly under your shouldrs. Keep your legs straight behind you, and your feet together.

2. Hold this position for as long as you can, working your way up to 60 seconds.

SCISSORS

Set/Time: 20-30 repetitions

1. Sit in a crunch posture with your legs extended up in a "scissors" position. Place your hands supportively behind your head.

2. Keeping your abs tight, inhale and exhale as you alternate moving your legs up and down, like a pair of scissors.

TWISTING CRUNCH

Set/Time: 20-30 repetitions

1. Sit in a crunch posture and hold your legs straight above the surface. Place your palms behind your head for support and keep your elbows wide and out of sight.

2. Keeping your abs tight, inhale and exhale as you twitch your arms and look to both your sides, back and forth.

STEP 5 – MILESTONES

"Remember to celebrate the milestones as you prepare for the road ahead."

-Nelson Mandela

When we think about big goals, dreams, or a point of change, unconsciously, we may start to get nervous and withdraw from the pursuit of the changes. This is a common biological response. According to the organizational theorist, Maasaki Inai (and based on the Japanese Kaizen philosophy), when we think about the great things that can happen to us, we get alarmed and shift to a defensive "fight or flight" stance. Even without noticing this occurrence, our motivation decreases and we begin to ignore the thoughts of change. This can happen to an even greater degree when we are taking actions that can propel change. This usually happens when we step out of our comfort zone.

"Stress of Change"

Coping Cycle

The comfort zone is a behavioral state in which a person operates in an anxiety-neutral condition, using a limited set of behaviors to deliver a steady level of performance, usually without a sense of risk. Change is not a single timed event, though. Change is a constant life event.

Every time a modification of behavior or performance occurs, a new change process begins and a new coping cycle commences, as well. Carnell's coping cycle is a valuable approach to understanding how people deal and cope with change. It illustrates the five main stages that people usually tend to go through during a behavioral change.

Stage 1 – "Denial"

When stepping outside the comfort zone, there are common feelings of anxiety and stress, accompanied by the resignation of leaving the current comfort zone. There is an increase of will to preserve the status quo and be happy with it.

Stage 2 – "Resistance"

There is a tendency to resist new things, and thus, there is increased clinging to practicing ancient customs and beliefs, as well as a desire to reject the change and to try to prove that it is not working or simply wrong.

Stage 3 – "Abandonment"

At this stage, there is a development which is focused on the present rather than the past, and a beginning of accepting and welcoming change. For example, people say, "I will probably have to give it a chance." This is the first phase of adaptation.

Stage 4 – "Adapting"

At this stage, there is acceptance of a new situation, and a sense of confidence in it. Most of the energy previously channeled to negative areas of resistance are now invigorating feelings of encouragement to settle the new situation and behavior.

Stage 5 – "Internalization"

This is the final stage, which provides us with a newly formed comfort zone. This is the phase with the highest sense of acceptance toward adapting a new kind of behavior and new habits.

One great technique for conquering this innate resistance to change, as well as better coping with "big" goals, is to break the target down to milestones, or "stepping stones."

When accomplishing my own ultramarathon races, I always found it more effective to focus on the closest targets that I could see and reach, like the next lap or the next rest station. This helped me continue my movement towards an otherwise seemingly endless goal. Without these mini-goals and empowering techniques, I am sure I would have broken down mentally.

If you look at your big target and feel overwhelmed, try to break it into smaller, more manageable pieces. This can be done in two ways.

The first way to manage seemingly overwhelming goals is to establish SMART milestones for your SMART goals. Just as you established SMART goals, break these goals into shorter and smaller segments. For example, if your goal in business is to gain $50,000 in revenue within a year, try breaking this down into quarterly segments, like

$10,000 in the first three months, $20,000 in the next five months, and $20,000 in the last four months.

The second way to use milestones is by setting SMART milestones for your action plan. For example, you can set milestones within your to-do list of tasks that you need to complete in order to accomplish each step of your action plan. By breaking your steps down into smaller steps, you will feel satisfaction and be motivated as you are able to check off your completed tasks.

Micro Goals

According to the Dominican University's "goal setting" research, which was undertaken in the educational field, dividing a long-term task into short-term goals (sub-goals or milestones) keeps student motivation high and leads to successful work completion towards the ultimate goal. One of the reasons for this effect is the feedback received on the long-term goal attainment process. Students in this research, and people in general, need to see progress toward their goals, especially when working to accomplish procedural goals.

A previous "Mental Representation of Progress" research study has also shown that the way people perceive the level of their progress on a goal will have a profound impact on their motivation. For example, when pursuing goals with specific endpoints, people are motivated by the progress that needs to be made in order for them to achieve goal attainment. People gain additional motivational boosts as they move closer to the endpoint of their pursuit. By reducing the amount of uncertainty, we are more encouraged to keep progressing.

"The soft-minded man always fears change. He feels security in the status quo, and he has an almost morbid fear of the new. For him, the greatest pain is the pain of a new idea."

-Martin Luther King

MILESTONES
TASK

Step 5 – Task

1. Set 3-5 milestones for your plan & goals!

You can view a YouTube presentation of these ideas here:

YOUR
EXERCISES
BAND

STEP 5 – MILESTONES: BAND EXERCISES

When thinking about a big goal, and especially when taking actions to achieve it, we may experience stress and anxiety, even without being aware of the causes.

❖ Stress is an unwanted feeling that most of us try to prevent or reduce, yet as we saw in this chapter, a right amount of stress can be helpful and plays a motivational role. We saw that one of the key techniques for coping with big goals that cause pressure is the method of breaking down the big target into smaller goals called "micro goals," better defined as "milestones."

❖ A great comparison to emphasize the importance of a right amount of stress to gain improvement and motivation is stretching band exercising. Only by pressuring our muscles to resist and to work harder can we gain a higher mass of muscles and build our body, just as by stretching our body parts, we become more flexible. Yet, it is important to be aware of not stressing our muscles' tension too much, as we do not want them to tear apart.

- ❖ Here is the fitness section of my band exercises that I encourage you to practice, at the level of your ability, so you improve your ability to cope with stressful goals, as well as improve your physical shape!

- ❖ **Disclaimer**: Consult with your physician or other health care professional before starting this or any other fitness program to determine if it is right for your needs. Do not start this fitness program if your physician or health care provider advises against it. If you experience faintness, dizziness, pain or shortness of breath at any time while exercising you should stop immediately.

STATIC LEG RESISTANCE

Set/Time: 10-15 seconds

3. Stand tall and attach the band around one ankle. Raise your active leg up with your knee bent and in line with your chest.

4. Inhale as you squeeze your elbows back, and simultaneously resist by pushing your foot forward against the tension of the band.

STANDING LEG EXTENSION

Set/Time: 10-20 repetitions (each side)

5. Stand tall and attach the band around one ankle. Raise your active leg up with your knee bent.

6. Straighten your active leg out in front of you until your knee is almost totally straight and hold in the new position for 3-5 seconds. Keep your elbows bent high and tighten your abs.

STANDING SIDE LEG EXTENSION

Set/Time: 5-15 repetitions (each side)

1. Stand tall and attach the band around one ankle. Raise your active leg up with your knee straight, and keep your heel perpendicular to the floor.

2. Hold the position with your leg in the air while maintaining balance and slowly open the leg straight to the side, setting a 90-degree angle. Inhale and hold there for a moment, then turn the leg back to the starting position.

ANKLE PRESS OUT

Set/Time: 10-15 repetitions (each side)

1. Stand tall with your feet close together. Put your palms on your hips for support.
2. Keeping your abs tight, exhale as you extend one leg outside in parallel line and widen your position. Hold for 5 seconds, and feel your hips tighten.

HIGH SHOULDERS BAND EXTENSION

Set/Time: 10-20 repetitions (each side)

1. Stand tall and hold the band in both palms. Raise your arms up above and beside your head, and have your elbows at a 45-degree angle.
2. Inhale and exhale as you repetitively and slightly deepen the squeezing of the band to the sides.

Ashmoret Mishal   Ultra Success | 130

BACK ARM EXTENSION

Set/Time: 10-20 repetitions (each side)

1. Stand straight with your left arm behind your back, holding the band at a 90-degree angle while bent.
2. Keeping your abs tight, exhale as you straighten your left elbow upward for a beat, and then bend it back again to the starting position.

QUADRUPED WITH LEG LIFT

Set/Time: 10-20 repetitions (each side)

1. Get down on your hands and knees with your palms flat on the floor and shoulder-width apart.

2. Wrap the band around your front knee and back foot. Without allowing your lower-back posture to change, raise your back leg, allowing a stretch of the band. Hold for 5-10 seconds, return to the starting position, and repeat the exercise again.

HIP RAISE WITH KNEE PRESS-OUT

Set/Time: 10-15 repetitions (each side)

1. Lie face up on the floor with your knees bent and your feet flat on the floor, supporting yourself with arms holding to the floor. Place the band just over your knees and keep them wide-apart.

2. Raise your hips so your body forms a straight line from your shoulders to your knees. Pause for up to 5 seconds in the up position, then lower your body back to the starting position.

STEP 6 – ABILITY AWARENESS

"At the center of your being you have the answer, you know who you are and you know what you want."

-Lao Tzu

"Nothing can stop anyone, if they are determined enough, and want something badly enough, while they are aware of the price of their choices, and that they are responsible for everything they choose to do.

"There are two types of goals: The first is a goal derived from social requirements and goals other people expect us to achieve, and then there are goals that are your own goals, which you choose and you generate.

"The more we learn about how to set goals for ourselves, which stem from our inner selves, goals we believe in and want to achieve, then, when we realize these goals that make us feel good we shall adapt this approach."

Excerpts from - I TRAIN FOR - Setting Goals, The North Face training video, Ashmoret Mishal, 2016.

"Few people can express with equanimity opinions which differ from the prejudices of their social environment. Most people are even incapable of forming such opinions."

-Albert Einstein

Understanding what motivates us and others in decision making, goal pursuits, and passion, is a major part of achieving our goals, and success can mainly be attributed to a high level of awareness and consciousness. Empowered people know their limits, and have a well-developed sense of self-awareness, which is a key quality for attaining success. Personal empowerment is about looking at who you are and becoming more aware of yourself as a unique individual.

Reflect upon yourself, and try honestly to identify your key strengths and weaknesses. Everyone has an inner "super power" – a powerful and influential trait or ability that you can use to your success. But on the flip side, it is just as important to identify your inner disadvantage – a trait that can harm your chances to succeed if you do not identify it and understand how to mitigate it. Becoming aware of your strengths and weaknesses is half the battle, and once you identify them, you can begin understanding how they will affect your goals.

The investment theory of intelligence proposes that interest is what drives people to invest their time and energy in developing skills and a base of knowledge. Interest precedes the development of talent. It turns out that motivation is the reason that people develop talent in the first place. Interest and drive are main components of "grit."

In his book, *Give and Take*, Adam Grant describes the importance of grit:

"The psychologist Angela Duckworth defines grit as 'having passion and perseverance toward long term goals.' Her research shows that, above and beyond intelligence and aptitude, people with grit achieve higher performance due to their interest, focus, and drive.

"Persistence is incredibly important. Of course, natural talent also matters, but once you have a pool of candidates above the threshold of necessary potential, grit is a factor that predicts how close they get to achieving their potential."

The following questionnaire is the Grit Scale, developed by Angela Duckworth. Once you finish answering the questions and grading yourself, calculate your score to understand how passionate and preserving you see yourself to be.

GRIT SCALE

1. I have overcome setbacks to conquer an important challenge.

- ○ Very much like me
- ○ Mostly like me
- ○ Somewhat like me
- ○ Not much like me
- ○ Not like me at all

2. New ideas and projects sometimes distract me from previous ones.

- ○ Very much like me
- ○ Mostly like me
- ○ Somewhat like me
- ○ Not much like me
- ○ Not like me at all

3. My interests change from year to year.

- ○ Very much like me
- ○ Mostly like me
- ○ Somewhat like me
- ○ Not much like me
- ○ Not like me at all

4. Setbacks don't discourage me. I don't give up easily.

○ Very much like me

○ Mostly like me

○ Somewhat like me

○ Not much like me

○ Not like me at all

5. I have been obsessed with a certain idea or project for a short time but later lost interest.

○ Very much like me

○ Mostly like me

○ Somewhat like me

○ Not much like me

○ Not like me at all

6. I am a hard worker.

○ Very much like me

○ Mostly like me

○ Somewhat like me

○ Not much like me

○ Not like me at all

7. I often set a goal but later choose to pursue a different one.

○ Very much like me

○ Mostly like me

○ Somewhat like me

○ Not much like me

○ Not like me at all

8. I have difficulty maintaining my focus on projects that take more than a few months to complete.

○ Very much like me

○ Mostly like me

○ Somewhat like me

○ Not much like me

○ Not like me at all

9. I finish whatever I begin.

○ Very much like me

○ Mostly like me

○ Somewhat like me

○ Not much like me

○ Not like me at all

10. I have achieved a goal that took years of work.

○ Very much like me

○ Mostly like me

○ Somewhat like me

○ Not much like me

○ Not like me at all

11. I become interested in new pursuits every few months.

○ Very much like me

○ Mostly like me

○ Somewhat like me

○ Not much like me

○ Not like me at all

12. I am diligent.

○ Very much like me

○ Mostly like me

○ Somewhat like me

○ Not much like me

○ Not like me at all

GRIT SCORING

For questions 1,4,6,9,10 and 12 assign the following points:

5 = Very much like me
4 = Mostly like me
3 = Somewhat like me
2 = Not much like me
1 = Not like me at all

For questions 2,3,5,7,8 and 11 assign the following points:

1 = Very much like me
2 = Mostly like me
3 = Somewhat like me
4 = Not much like me
5 = Not like me at all

Add up all the points and divide by 12. The maximum score on this scale is 5 (extremely gritty), and the lowest scale on this scale is 1 (not at all gritty).

" THE KEY TO GET AHEAD IS TO GET STARTED "

Coach Henry Gregory

When describing potential, it is very common for us to misjudge our strengths and weaknesses. This can lead to feelings of inability, or on the contrary, defiance against actual limitations. Therefore, it is essential to accurately understand the personal strengths and weaknesses we have in order to fulfill our real potential.

We will further discuss the persistence quality in Step 8 of the method. For now, go ahead and list 3 personal weaknesses and 3 personal strengths that can affect and influence your goals achievement process and success. Then, identify your main "super-power" and your main disadvantage. Lastly, decide what you need to improve the most, and how you will empower your "super-power", disadvantage or both. For example, some of the entrepreneurs I work with will point out that their leadership skills are strong, but their management skills are weak. In order to be practical and effective, we need to be very specific and ask: "what kind of management skills do I need to improve?" Also, it is important that we be very specific in the different actions we will take to become better.

Not only is it important to be self-aware on the personal level, but it is also a key for success in business. Research from 2010 concluded that, among interpersonal traits of 72 top companies' executives, the one trait which resonated the most, and the one with the strongest predictor for overall success, was self-awareness:

> "Interestingly, a high self-awareness score was the strongest predictor of overall success. This is not altogether surprising as executives who are aware of their weaknesses are often better able to hire subordinates who perform well in categories in which the leader lacks acumen. These leaders are also more able to entertain the idea that someone on their team may have an idea that is even better than their own."

> -Dr. Winkler, Green Peak Partners

Managers and leaders who are self-aware are better able to identify their own strengths and weaknesses, and therefore are able to find, hire, and mentor high potential employees who complement their strengths and weaknesses, therefore resulting in better overall business performance. This is one way to lessen the liability of a disadvantage on your business's success.

ABILITY AWARENESS TASK

Step 6 – Task

1. List your personal strengths and weaknesses regarding your goals.

2. Write down your "super-power" and main disadvantage that can affect your goal-related performance.

3. Write down the actions you need to take to improve the chosen qualities or skills.

STEP 6 – SELF-AWARENESS: BALANCING EXERCISES

A key part of being a high achiever and becoming more successful is a matter of training and focus. Yet, sustained concentration and attention to your goals may sometimes interfere with your balance in other fields and aspects of life, such as family, friendship, relationships, physical health, wellness, and more.

❖ Being self-aware of your own goals and needs, and finding the right balance between them — and moreover having awareness of balancing your mates, family, and close friends — is a difficult task. As you focus too much on one goal, it distracts you from other goals and needs. If you only concentrate closely on one target and dedicate your life to it, other parts of your life may fade away, as there is a return to each investment and thus each lack of investment.

❖ For many of us who are too motivated, our struggle can be to find the ideal balance point. This can also be true for those of us who have lack motivation – it's essential to find the other side of the ultimate balance point. Therefore, I've provided you the fitness section of my balancing exercises that I encourage you to practice, at the level of your ability, so you may improve your stability, as well as improve your physical shape!

❖ **Disclaimer**: Consult with your physician or other health care professional before starting this or any other fitness program to determine if it is right for your needs. Do not start this fitness program if your physician or health care provider advises against it. If you experience faintness, dizziness, pain or shortness of breath at any time while exercising you should stop immediately.

QUADRUPED WITH LEG LIFT

Set/Time: hold pose for 30-60 seconds

1. Shift your weight onto your left leg and press the bottom of your right foot onto your right thigh.

2. Stay here for at least 30 seconds before repeating on the other side.

TREE, HANDS HIGH

Set/Time: hold pose for 15-30 seconds

1. Shift your weight onto your right leg and press the bottom of your left foot onto your right thigh. Press your palms together above your head.

2. Stay here for at least 12 seconds, trying to close your eyes and focus on your stability. Then, repeat on the other side.

HIGH LUNGE ARM UP

Set/Time: hold pose for 15-30 seconds (each side)

1. Stand with your feet shoulder-width apart, your weight on your heels. Lift your left leg and step in an elongated stride.

2. As your foot touches the floor, bend your leading left knee, keeping your hips low and raising your left arm high, pointed to the sky.

KNEELING BALANCE

Set/Time: 15-30 repetitions (each side)

1. Start on all fours with your hands directly under your shoulders and your knees directly under your hips.
2. Maintaining your balance, slowly reach out with your right arm as you push through the hell to extend your right leg in the opposite direction. You should feel like you are stretching both ways.

QUADRUPED WITH LEG LIFT

Set/Time: 15-30 seconds (each side)

1. Stand tall with your feet and legs straight and wide apart. Lean your torso forward over your front leg, keeping both sides of your torso long.

2. Reset your right hand on your shin or ankle, and lean back-opening your shoulders and extending the left arm up above your shoulder. Look up to your left fingers.

EASY SIDE BEND

Set/Time: 15-30 seconds (each side)

1. Stand with your feet wide apart, inhale, and reach your right arm out and up above your head, with a slight tilt of your hip to the left side.
2. Stay here for at least 15 seconds and then repeat on the other side.

QUADRICEPS STRETCH

Set/Time: 15-30 seconds (each side)

1. Stand tall and curl your leg up behind you. Grab your foot with one or two hands.
2. Keeping your knees apart, stretch your leg backward, opening your chest.

TRICEPS BENCH DIPS

Set/Time: 10-20 seconds

1. Sit on the edge of a low bench or stair and walk your legs forward so that only your heels touch the floor and your arms support your weight.
2. Keeping your abs tight, inhale and exhale as you hold position.

STEP 7 – CHALLENGING

"Don't handicap your children by making their lives easy."

-Robert A. Heinlein

Challenges are tasks which require great mental or physical effort in order to prevail successfully. Some people tend to seek out challenges, and as soon as they succeed, they move on and look for new challenges. Usually, these people function well in high-pressure situations or environments, because pressure and challenges improve their performance. Other people would prefer to stay away from challenges and will do whatever it takes to avoid them. They do this because the challenge – which can be caused by any parameter of time, competition, complication, etc. – would put them under too much stress, impeding their performance.

Research conducted by psychologists Robert Yerkes and John Dodson has shown that there is a direct relationship between pressure and performance. When people experience the right amount of pressure, they deliver their best work. However, if there is too much pressure (over-challenging) or too little pressure (under-challenging), then performance is liable to suffer and decline. This is called the "Inverted U model." This model is also known as the Yerkes-Dodson Law.

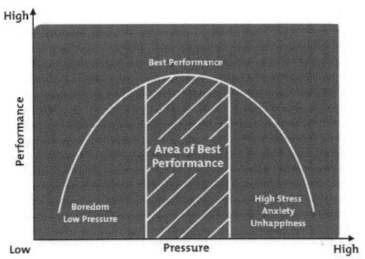

Too much pressure can affect our performance in a negative way due to stress, just as a lack of pressure can lead to complacency, frozen in the same place, without making any progress. The technique of using small steps, or Milestones, as discussed in Chapter 5, is effective in combatting the negative effects of too much pressure. By following a step by step progression, we can overcome stress and train ourselves to conquer it, thus, eventually taking control of the situation.

By facing daily challenges and adopting them as a way of life, we are able to develop and build confidence. Confidence is one of the greatest motivators and most powerful limitation-eliminators for those who want to change their behavior and become more empowered.

So, what kind of challenges should we choose? It is essential to identify challenges that are meaningful for us, and to find some meaning in the challenge we face. For example, this could mean finding goals that suit our beliefs and values. As Dr. Gail Matthews from Dominican University found, goals should be meaningful and valuable if students are to achieve their goals. If students do not perceive their challenges as meaningful or valuable, their engagement with the goal attainment progress will be diminished.

It has also been found that challenges are particularly important for the enjoyment of intrinsically motivated and goal oriented activities. Challenges also imbue a true feeling of competence in participants. This relates to the "grit" quality described in the Chapter 6, and is directly linked to success, as defined by Tony Robbins in his book, *Unlimited Power*:

> "Often we get caught in the mental trap of seeing enormously successful people and thinking they are where they are because they

have some special gift. Yet a closer look shows that the greatest gift that extraordinarily successful people have over the average person is to get themselves to act. It's a 'gift' that any of us can develop within ourselves."

What is the best way to practice the necessary skills?

Business professor Andrew Johnston uses marathon training to fuel his students' successes. In the program titled, "Change Through Challenge," at Red Rocks Community College outside of Denver, Colorado, Johnston's students participate to earn college credit. There, Johnston teaches the skills and values of goal achievement in practical ways. For 21 weeks, students, many of whom have never run before, meet twice a week – Monday nights in a classroom, and Saturday mornings on a running trail – to learn about goal setting, setbacks, perseverance, and, ultimately, the triumph of completion. The final exam: the Rock 'n' Roll Marathon in Phoenix.

Review my interview with Andrew:

♦ How did you come up with the ideas of combining a marathon preparation course with the syllabus of business school?

"The genesis of the idea was in 2010 when I first started teaching. I was shocked at the low rate of student retention and completion for two and four year schools (approximately 30% and 54% respectively). I noticed most students didn't quit school due to lack of <u>intelligence</u>, but lack of <u>GRIT</u>."

"I was trying to come up with an idea to teach grit that was more practical than the typical seminar or textbook. One day (on a run of course) I was reminded how marathon training helped me through the darkest times in my life (such as getting laid off and nearly losing everything back in 2009) and it was at that moment it occurred to me that marathon training would be the ideal vehicle to teach grit."

♦ What is the most important lesson that you teach young entrepreneurs through your marathon courses?

"Each week we discuss a "discipline of the week" (e.g. goal setting) and how that discipline related to their training also relates to their schoolwork, business and life in general. As it is a 22-week course, we discuss 22 disciplines. Of all the disciplines, I think the most powerful discipline is the power of <u>CONSISTENCY</u>. We discuss that going 26.2 miles on race day requires the student to train not just on the days s/he feels like it, but also on the days s/he DOESN'T feel like it. We relate how this concept holds true in succeeding at the highest level in ANY endeavor: you don't earn a degree by studying on just the days you feel like studying, but on the days you DON'T feel like studying, you don't become a top sales person by making cold calls on the days you feel like making cold calls, you become a top sales person by making calls on the days you don't feel like it. The examples are endless."

♦ Please share with us some of your examples and experiences that reflect the same kind of challenges which your students face in both the long- distance running field, and the business field.

"My students come from all walks of life facing diverse challenges—everything from the young single mom working full-time while pursuing her degree to escape poverty to the professional couple seeking to enhance their marriage to the 30-year old single dad re-entering society after a period of incarceration."

♦ What is your course's most memorable success / change story?

"One of my most memorable experiences was a story I mentioned in my TED Talk. It was a high school counselor named Sandy. Sandy signed up for the course while recovering from hip surgery. Due to the surgery, Sandy had been unable to exercise for over a year and was, as a result, not in the best of shape. Despite this setback, Sandy persevered with the training in hopes of personal renewal and to dedicate the marathon to her mom who had recently died. Sandy was the model of CONSISTENCY in that every week she would execute the training (especially the Saturday long runs) by walking for several minutes then running several minutes, mile after mile, week after week for 22 weeks. This consistency allowed Sandy to not only cross the marathon finish line, but do it under the 7-hour cut-off. She also lost over 30 pounds during the training. Again, a model of how CONSISTENT effort can yield amazing results."

♦ Is your program scalable, by measuring its correlation with success or grit?

"I absolutely think the program is scalable as the concepts are simple and, in my opinion, nothing new. I am actually working on creating a text along with instructor resources so others can implement the program in THEIR school. The marathon, in my opinion, is the perfect vehicle to develop grit and resilience in people but I think there are other vehicles (e.g. bike race) that can yield the same results. It's all about forcing people to get used to facing their demons, dig deep and ask themselves to do more than they ever have. When people get used to asking more of themselves, they develop HABITS that not only allow them to conquer the marathon, but conquer OTHER challenges (e.g. earning a degree, starting a business) in life."

Unlike a running competition – where, after 4, 14, 24, or 38 hours of running, the competition ends after you cross the finish line – running a business does not have a clear finish line. You keep moving all the time, and you never stop 'running' your business. I compare managing a business to a daily marathon, or an endless ultra-marathon, especially at the beginning.

The same challenges that I faced in running are the same challenges that I face in business. Sometimes you feel as if you are hitting a wall, that you don't have any more energy, or as if you are on a roller-coaster with highs and lows. You may want to quit and give up because suddenly it is too much to handle.

The same qualities that helped me to run for 14 or 24 or 38 hours are the same qualities that helped me to keep moving my business forward.

You might now be wondering: How can exercise and running be used as a metaphor that is going to improve my business and personal life?

Here is the explanation:

- ❖ Exercise and running contain many of the same challenges that you encounter at work and in your personal life. Therefore, you must take the essential lessons needed for successful running and apply these to improving your business skills:

- ❖ PLANNING is essential to running—just as it is to work and your life out of the office.

- ❖ SELF-CONTROL is required for running—and for success in business and your personal life.

- ❖ OVERCOMING CHALLENGES is a key part of running—and is relevant for work and home life.

- ❖ CONSISTENCY is important in running—as it is in your professional and personal life.

- ❖ FOCUS is critical for running—and equally significant for business and life outside of work.

❖ CRISIS MANAGEMENT is vital for running—and, of course, is crucial for both corporate and personal life.

In Step 9 we will discuss the actual skills and tools that we teach and practice to achieve any business, personal, or sport long-term goals. But for now, in Step 7, the key is understanding that we can apply the skills we have discussed in Steps 1 through 6 to our current challenges. In particular, we must be flexible to changes, act with creative thinking, and use Steps 1 through 5 to better manage the process of problem-solving.

CHALLENGE
TASK

Step 7 – Task

1. Write down your current and future challenges and come up with problem solving strategies and solutions.
2. Identify your ultimate pressure point for your peak performance.

STEP 7 – CHALLENGING: BOSU BALANCING EXERCISES

Challenging yourself along the way to achieving your goals and overcoming the challenges that you face you face are important and valuable skills. There are endless types of physical challenges in business that relate to human resources, financial resources, limitations, bureaucracy, and more. Yet, the challenges that I believe are the most essential to tackle are mental challenges, which relate to each in the following way:

1. Uncertainty – Fear of the Unknown

2. Loss of Faith – Pessimistic Mindset

3. Loss of Grip – Passive Actions

❖ For a majority of people, uncertainty is horrifying and frustrating. When it is present in high levels, it may lead to pessimism and later to passivism, if we do not overcome it in its earliest stages. Remember that none of the most successful people or start-ups in the world knew with 100% certainty that they would be successful. Yet, what they did have was an extreme amount of hope, optimism, and faith.

❖ Therefore, I am providing the fitness section of my Bosu-ball exercises that will shake your stability and grip. This will encourage you to cope with the challenge both physically and mentally, at the level of your ability, so that you can improve your mind-focus and stamina, as well as improve your physical shape!

❖ **Disclaimer**: Consult with your physician or other health care professional before starting this or any other fitness program to determine if it is right for your needs. Do not start this fitness program if your physician or health care provider advises against it. If you experience faintness, dizziness, pain or shortness of breath at any time while exercising you should stop immediately.

DANCER

Set/Time: hold pose for 5-10 seconds (each side)

1. Stand tall on the bosu. Shift your weight onto your right leg. Reach your right arm up while slowly raising your back leg in a line with your hand.

2. Exhale as you gently press your right foot onto the bosu to maintain balance, and repeat this exercise again.

TREE POSE

Set/Time: hold pose for 5 seconds (each side)

1. Stand tall on a bosu ball with your hands behind your head. Shift your weight onto your left leg and press the bottom of your right foot onto your right tibia.

2. Stay here for at least 5 seconds and try the same thing on the other side.

SQUAT

Set/Time: hold pose for 5-10 seconds

1. Stand tall on the bosu with your feet close together. Imagine you are about to take a seat. Inhale as you bend our legs and lower your hips until your thighs are almost parallel to the floor.
2. Bring your arms to 90 degrees from the floor and look forward. Bend your back slightly and hold this position.

HIP RAISE

Set/Time: hold pose for 5-10 seconds

1. In a reversed plank, place your arms on the bosu ball. Keep your legs straight forward and gently elevate your hips.

2. Exhale and hold in this position, keeping shoulders in a straight line with your knees and feet. Pause up to 10 seconds and repeat the exercise again.

PUSH-UP

Set/Time: 10-15 repetitions

1. Sit down in a leg spread with your palms forward. Slowly raise yourself so you lean against the bosu, pressing it with your palms. Keep your eyes looking forward.

2. Inhale as you tighten your abs and slowly straighten your elbows to a push-up position. Repeat this exercise as many times as you can.

PLANK

Set/Time: hold pose for 15-30 seconds

1. Start in a push-up position. Place your hands flat on the surface, elbows directly under your shoulders. Keep your legs straight behind you, and your feet together on top of the bosu.

2. Hold this position for as long as you can, working your way up to 30 seconds.

KNEES STANDING

Set/Time: hold pose for 15-30 seconds

1. On the bosu, stand on your knees with your feet pointing above the floor. Place your hands behind your back.

2. Exhale as you gently press your right foot onto the bosu to maintain balance, and hold in the position.

BOSU SIDE TILT

Set/Time: hold pose for 15-30 seconds

1. Stand tall while holding a bosu ball above your head.

2. Slightly tilt your hips to the side, keeping your legs hip width apart. Hold there for a moment, and slowly come back to the starting position.

STEP 8 – PERSISTENCE

"In the beginner's mind, there are many possibilities, but in the expert's mind there are few."

-Shunryu Suzuki

Well-being is a term used in psychology to describe a person's subjective assessment of their overall quality of life and mental health. Many people around the world suffer from a low level of well-being. Studies have found that one of the main contributors to a healthy well-being is physical exercise. It has been observed that physical exercise improves one's mood, as well as reduces symptoms of stress, anger, depression, and anxiety. Studies have also shown that physical activity is associated with higher levels of happiness and satisfaction in life. In contrast, a lack of exercise is associated with high levels of anxiety and depression. Yet, it is still unclear whether the lack of physical activity causes depression or whether depression causes physical inactivity.

Another study has found that self-confidence is one of the parameters associated with mental well-being, and that participating in physical exercise contributes significantly to the development and improvement of self-confidence. This finding suggests that aerobic exercise improves self-esteem, and probably also has an antidepressant effect. Building self-esteem is highly important from a health perspective: it is essential to emotional stability and any adaptation to the necessities of life. Moreover, another important quality relating to self-esteem is body image. Several studies have found that physical activity among men and women leads them to assess their physical appearance at a higher level, and they are then significantly more satisfied with various aspects of their bodies, unlike people who are less physically active.

Although most people understand that they should participate in physical activity, many have a low level of self-discipline regarding their physicality. A few years ago, I was asked to train a group of executives for a major corporation in Israel. The group consisted of fifty managers, with ages ranging from 40 to 60. The training period lasted nine months, with a training session scheduled once per week. The purpose of this group training was to improve the managers' health, shape, and productivity. At the first session, everyone showed up! I was ecstatic; we had 100% attendance. But slowly there was a decline in the attendance, and ultimately nearly 75% "dropped out," on average, across ten different cities the same project took place at.

Another example that demonstrates the challenge of persistence and consistency in training is healthcare programs for clients who receive a personal trainer for ten classes. On average, most of the trainees barely make it to the fifth class. The dropout numbers are staggering! Although it is not impossible to achieve long-term goals such as losing weight or succeeding in sports without a high level of discipline, it will undoubtedly lead to greater results if we practice and train with discipline. Self-discipline is a habit, a practice, a philosophy, and a way of life. All successful men and women are highly disciplined when it comes to the important work that they do.

According to the article, *Self-Discipline Outdoes IQ in Predicting Academic Performance of Adolescents,* by Angela L. Duckworth and Martin E.P. Seligman, in the *Psychological Science Journal*, self-discipline is a better predictor of academic success than even IQ.

All great successes in life are preceded by extended, sustained periods of focused effort towards a single goal, the most important goal, with the determination to stick with it until success is fulfilled. Persistence is an extraordinary trait, and it is a key predictor of whether you will succeed or fail in your long-term goals, regardless of whether it is a physical or entrepreneurial goal. It would be near impossible to go out and run a marathon without consistent and persistent training beforehand, just as it would be near impossible to launch a successful business without advanced preparation beforehand.

Success Starts In Movement

ULTRA LEADERSHIP METHOD

Throughout history, we have seen that every man or woman who achieved anything lasting and worthwhile has engaged in long and often unappreciated hours, weeks, months, or sometimes even years of concentrated, disciplined work, often aimed in a single specific direction. Once you have mastered the ability to postpone instant gratification, having the ability to discipline yourself to stay focused on the most important task ahead of you, there is virtually no goal that you cannot accomplish and no task that you cannot complete.

"People who have attained excellence follow a consistent path to success."

-Tony Robbins

PERSISTENCE
TASK

Step 8 – Task

1. Grade your persistent based on the grit scale of Step 6.

2. Identify which of your persistence skills or habits you
   need to improve and how.

YOUR EXERCISES
LEGS

STEP 8 – PERSISTENCE: LEGS EXERCISES

The main mantra of the Ultra Leadership Method is "Success Starts in Movement." Being physically in movement will lead you to your goal's "finish line." There are no short-cuts in long-term success, so we always need to be moving and pushing ourselves further. The motivational drive of running towards your goal Is irreplaceable, and is one of the best motivators available, especially at the beginning of our path.

❖ We all know that it takes significant effort to achieve our goals, but it is much harder to achieve it by ourselves. It is tiring and sometimes so exhausting that we may think about quitting.

❖ Therefore, I have provided you with the fitness section of my leg exercises that will make your legs so strong, so you will not have excuses to stop running and moving toward achieving your goals.

❖ **Disclaimer:** Consult with your physician or other health care professional before starting this or any other fitness program to determine if it is right for your needs. Do not start this fitness program if your physician or health care provider advises against it. If you experience faintness, dizziness, pain or shortness of breath at any time while exercising you should stop immediately.

BASIC LUNGE

Set/Time: hold pose for 15-30 repetitions (each side)

1. Stand with your feet wide apart. Lift your right leg and step forward.

2. Once your foot touches the floor, bend your back knee toward the floor. Then, stepping back into the starting position, repeat on the other side.

HIGH LUNGE

Set/Time: hold pose for 30 seconds (each side)

1. Stand with your feet wide apart. Lift your right leg and step forward onto a higher surface.

2. Keeping your abs tight, exhale as you hold in the static position where your back knee is straight, standing tall with your hands straight up.

LEG PRESS

Set/Time: hold pose for 30 seconds (each side)

1. Stand with your feet wide apart. Lift your left leg and step backward with your foot pressing the wall, with your knee pointed.

2. Once your foot touches the floor, stretch your position with your hands extended high and across from your body.

SPIDER

Set/Time: hold pose for 30 seconds (each side)

1. Sit down with your knees bent to the floor. Place your hands beside you, across from your legs, keeping elbows out straight.

2. Keeping your abs tight, exhale as you roll up your right leg, with its foot pushing against the wall. Keep your chin high and look forward.

SQUAT

Set/Time: hold pose for 15-30 seconds

1. Stand tall with your feet close together. Imagine you are about to take a seat. Inhale as you bend your legs and lower your hips until your thighs are almost parallel to the floor.

2. Bring your arms to 90 degrees from the floor and look forward. Bend your back slightly and hold this position.

SIDE KICK

Set/Time: hold pose for 30 seconds (each side)

1. Stand with your feet wide apart. Lift your left leg, pointed out and with 90 degrees (or more) away from the surface).

2. Hold your arms together close to your chest, and hold the posture while breathing deeply.

SINGLE KNEE HUG

Set/Time: hold pose for 20-40 repetitions (each side)

1. Stand tall with your feet wide apart. Lift your right leg, bent above your hip, with your knee close to your chest.

2. Once your knee is pointed up, hold it with your left hand for support, and bring your leg close to your chest. Then stepping back into the starting position, repeat on the other side.

FRONT KICK

Set/Time: hold pose for 30 seconds (each side)

1. Stand tall with your feet wide apart. Lift your right leg straight in a kick move above your hip, across your chest.

2. Once your foot is pointed out straight, hold the position for as long as half a minute, with a light hip-twist.

"Among the great things which are to be found among us,
the being of nothingness is the greatest."

-Leonardo Da Vinci

"When you're at your most difficult point, when you are at a crossroads and you must decide whether to continue or back down, that is when the real test begins. Running long distances – is also a kind of education. It is an anthology of life lessons, of knowing how to set yourself a goal, knowing how to plan how to achieve that goal.

"Perseverance, fine-tuning your self-discipline. And even the little things – when we are tired and have no energy, and it's hot or cold or raining, we get out there because we've set ourselves a goal, and that is part of that discipline – making rules for yourself and sticking with them and coping with the difficulty.

"Like when it gets hard in the middle of a session, and you want to give up, and then you say; 'No, I'm not stopping, I'm not giving up.' To generate this kind of discipline, you must remind yourself that it is something that you want, that it's important to you, that there was a reason you chose it, and the moment you identify the true reason you chose the goal – you need to start working.

"One of the physical exercises, which is also a mental exercise, is defining a goal which I know will be challenging for me, and which will make the session more difficult for me. It could be, for example, if I'm standing in front of a long staircase, then I can choose to set a goal for myself, such as: 'I am going to run here for fifteen minutes straight', and go up and down, up and down, up and down, and I know that after 7 or 8 minutes I'll be dead tired.

"But I won't stop there and give up – I'll keep on going, and I'll keep going up and down, and I'll repeat it multiple times until it becomes automatic. It doesn't require much thought, because you're already there, you're immersed in it, and all you need is to see that time is moving forward, and that you're fine, that it will be over soon."

Excerpts from - I TRAIN FOR – Discipline, The North Face training video, Ashmoret Mishal, 2016:

Through physical and endurance training, we can adapt and improve our coping strategies and tools to overcome challenges and difficulties. These tools are not just for physical challenges, but also professional ones. Just as you can "work out" your heart in exercise to build physical stamina, you can also build emotional stamina through practice. There are two categories of coping techniques and strategies in the Ultra Leadership Method: physical tools and mental tools. There are three physical tools that are ways to gain and improve self- control, relaxation, and perseverance. There are also four mental tools that are mindfulness techniques to help overcome difficult moments, events, and setbacks.

Let's begin with the physical techniques.

Breathe!

When entering the world of monotonous running, there is often not much stimulation to distract from the physical effort felt through rapid heart rates, sweating, and huffing. Those physiological symptoms often cause mental stress or anxiety, which are translated to the subconscious as danger signs. Therefore, you should try to adapt a monotonous breathing technique in order to relax the physiological symptoms and, correspondingly, mental symptoms of stress.

'Small Steps' Jogging

Adapting a light technique – preserving energy and continuity of movement – is helpful in difficult training moments. Rather than stopping or quitting, we can find alternative or "smoother" solutions. If the situation is very stressful and impedes the level of efficiency and performance, we should maintain the right amount of volume to have enough energy to accomplish the task or goal.

"The journey of a thousand miles begins with a single step."

-Chinese Proverb

'Head up', Looking Forward

Usually during a challenging workout, the body becomes very tired. Automatically and unconsciously, we tend to bow our head down, looking at the floor. In these moments, we should pay attention to this tendency and raise our chin up instead for two primary reasons:

The first reason is physiological. When the chin is held high, more oxygen enters the lungs, which assists in aerobic exercising. The second reason is mental. Head down positioning can lead to a pessimistic sensation, but when we look up and straight forward, we can see the "light at the end of the tunnel," and leading us to be more goal-oriented and positive. This motivation is important because willpower is essential to accomplish the challenge.

And now to discuss the mental coping techniques.

Internal Dialogue

Many of us experience negative thought patterns and self-sabotaging fallacies that come up during a tough exercise or hard times. "I can't do it anymore," "It's not for me," and so on. To deal with these thoughts, we can use the tool of internal dialogue to negate these negative thoughts with positive feedback. We will reply to these thoughts in an optimistic manner, "Yes, I can!", "I love it!"

Positive Reinforcement

Self-encouragement is important when it comes to decision-making. When dealing with a crisis, I highly recommend that you try to avoid feeling embarrassed, and tell yourself words of positive reinforcement: "I am strong," "I am able." The positive language and feedback, as well as self-awareness of what we feel, is critical to our success.

Visualization

Visualization, or imagining, is one of the most significant tools for coping with crises. One of the most challenging aspects of running long distances or trying to achieve long-term goals is that we don't see the "finish line," either visually or metaphorically. I usually imagine encouraging things when I cannot literally see the finish line, such as what the finish line looks like, or the good feeling that I get after I finish a competition. Imagination helps build a sense of reality.

Milestones

One of the biggest challenges when pursuing big goals is that they can seem distant and impossible, so much so that we may want to give up many times during the process, sometimes even before trying. Therefore, you should take the big goal and break it down into milestones (as discussed in Step 5 – Milestones), which can be more easily seen realistically and mentally. Whenever you're concentrating on the upcoming next goal and micro-goal, this strategy helps you reach them. Once you reach it, you set a new micro goal. Just as in the physical tool, "small steps, jog," you should think about the small steps towards success, rather than concentrating solely on the final point.

Meaning in Life

When we set goals and achieve them, this usually results in a higher sense of internal "locus of control," self-realization, and a sense of meaning in life. "Locus of control" is the degree to which people believe that they have control over the outcome of events in their lives, as opposed to external forces beyond their control. Individuals with a strong internal locus of control believe that events in their life are derived primarily from their own actions.

When people tend towards consistently conquering their goals, they fulfill a psychological need related to a sense of meaning in life. Feelings of fulfillment affect them on the physiological holistic experience, so that eventually they may feel a higher sense of having a meaningful life.

A sense of meaning in life is related to the fulfillment of the four psychological needs of the person: reason, value, self-value, and self-efficacy value. A person's self-efficacy is often measured by the goals that set that they have chosen for themselves and those that they have or have not achieved during their lifetime.

In his book from 1963, *Man's Search for Meaning*, Viktor Frankl claims that people are strongly motivated to find personal meaning in their lives, and that this is mainly due to a desire to understand the nature of their lives, to feel that their lives are meaningful and important rather than mundane and unimportant, and to feel that they have something to offer to others living in the world.

Going back to our discussion in Step 1 – "Setting a Goal," you can use this idea of setting a meaningful goal to help you to overcome crisis and difficult moments. There are always going to be excuses to quit and to stop when obstacles arise, but knowing that you are working towards something significant and meaningful will help you succeed in your long- term goals. People on a mission usually get things done!

C R I S I S
M A N A G E M E N T
T A S K

Step 9 Task

1. Write down your current or possible future crises and describe how you will overcome them or prevent them from happening.

2. Decide which helpful coping techniques you shall improve, adopt or practice.

YOUR EXERCISES
DUMBBELLS

STEP 9 – CRISIS MANAGEMENT: DUMBBELLS

EXERCISES

Crisis is an event that can threaten a person's stability and safety. Crisis Management is one of the most important qualities of ultramarathon runners, as they put themselves in expected conditions of extreme challenges that may lead to crises.

But these types of events are not just frequent in endurance sports, of course, but also in life, business, and work, as well. So, it is essential that you be able to overcome these crises as they arise.

Therefore, I have provided you the fitness section of my dumbbells exercises that will empower your body and mind to overcome the force resistance of external objects and events, and to maintain better control.

♦ Disclaimer: Consult with your physician or other health care professional before starting this or any other fitness program to determine if it is right for your needs. Do not start this fitness program if your physician or health care provider advises against it. If you experience faintness, dizziness, pain or shortness of breath at any time while exercising you should stop immediately.

TRICEPS PRESS

Set/Time: hold pose for 10-15 seconds

1. Stand tall with a dumbbell in each hand, feet shoulder width apart. Exhale as you pull the dumbbell up to your hip.
2. Pause, then inhale as you lower the dumbbell back to the starting point.

SINGLE TRICEPS PRESS

Set/Time: 15 repetitions (each side)

1. Place one foot forward into a light lunge and support yourself by placing your free hand on the bent knee. Square up your shoulder and hips, and lock yourself into a strong position.
2. Exhale as you pull the dumbbell up to your hip with your back elbow in a 90-degree angle. Pause and then inhale as you lower the dumbbell back to the starting position.

EXTENDING TRICEPS PRESS

Set/Time: hold pose for 30 seconds (each side)

1. Stand with your feet wide apart and step forward with your left leg so the knee is directly over the ankle. Your back leg should be completely straight. Hold a dumbbell in your right hand with your palms facing backward.

2. Press the weight back behind you as far as you can, maintaining a straight arm throughout the entire movement.

ANTERIOR SHOULDER RAISE

Set/Time: 10-15 repetitions

1. Stand tall with your feet shoulder width apart. Your arms should be at your sides, a dumbbell in each hand.

2. Slowly raise the dumbbells up in front of your body to chest level with your palms facing down. Exhale and lower down the dumbbells, back down to the starting position.

SHOULDER PRESS

Set/Time: 20 repetitions

1. Hold dumbbells in your hands against your chest. Slowly push the weight plate straight up until your arms are fully extended.
2. Hold for a beat, then retract your limbs back to the starting position.

STATIC SHOULDER PRESS

Set/Time: hold pose for 10 seconds

1. Hold dumbbells in your hands against your chest. Slowly push the weight plates straight up until your arms are fully extended.

2. Stay here for 10 seconds and breathe deeply, keeping your elbows slightly bent.

LATERAL SHOULDER EXTENSION

Set/Time: 15-20 repetitions

1. Start your exercise with your dumbbells raised up in front of your body in line with your chest. Hold your weights in both hands, touching each other.
2. Exhale and slowly lift the weights out and to the side with your palms facing down.
3. Hold for a beat and slowly move your arms back to the starting position.

PUSH-UPS ON TOES AND DUMBBELLS

Set/Time: hold pose for 10 seconds

1. With your arms straight and wider than shoulder width apart, support your body on dumbbells and toes. Your toes can be hip width apart or together.
2. Inhale as you bend your arms and lower your upper body 4 inches. Hold in the position for up to 10 seconds.

STEP 10 – STATUS CONTROL

"If a man wishes to be sure of the road he treads on, he must close his eyes and walk in the dark."

-St. John of the Cross

Revisiting our progress and condition is important to ensuring our success in achieving our chosen goals. It is essential to be focused and goal-oriented, and it is a vital and key action to keep track of our ongoing path and journey. In checking that we are still going in the right direction, we must be able to adapt to changes at the same time. In other words, we must be willing and able to reset our goals if necessity arises.

Flexible leadership is the extent to which a leader's behavior varies in appropriate ways to the different tasks they need to tackle with their subordinates. Flexibility in the case of one's own self-leadership is primarily required when changes occur over time in a subordinate's skills and motivation. When a sudden, unusual, or harmful event threatens to disrupt our normal condition, we should take the appropriate measures to minimize the repercussions.

How well a leader handles these immediate crises is an indicator of flexible and adaptive leadership. Over a longer period, major changes in the external environment create emerging threats or opportunities for the organization, and changes in strategies or tactics are often needed to ensure the effective performance and continued survival of the organization.

Strong management requires a "keeping all options open" approach, and that's where your contingency planning comes in. Contingency planning involves identifying alternative courses of action that can be implemented when the original plan proves inadequate due to changes in circumstances. Anticipating possible changes during the planning process is ideal in case things do not go as expected. Management can then develop alternatives to the existing plan and prepare them for use, when and if circumstances make these alternatives appropriate.

Flexible and effective leaders will find a suitable balance between the need for accomplishment and reassessment. This is the right way to avoid negative implications that could emerge from the new threat or condition. One of the ways to be flexible is to find substitutes. For example, during hard training for a marathon, someone might injure his- or herself from over-training. This is an example of a tension between the need for accomplishment – finishing the race – and the right way of avoiding negative outcomes, potentially risking the health and ability to run again. As described above, an example of flexible solutions may mean signing up for a shorter distance race, running for a lower rank, or signing up on different date.

It is important to remember that managing professional or business goals is different than personal goals, like training for a marathon or losing weight. Business goals can be affected by market fluctuations, external limitations, and the decisions and actions of other players. We may find that we need to adjust ourselves accordingly in the face of these changes, but it is important to try to stay as close to the original goal and plan as possible.

In her book, *If Success is the Game, These are the Rules*, Cherie Carter-Scott describes the process of goal attainment, with its upcoming changes:

> "You cannot know the sweetness of success unless you have tasted the bitterness of failure. You cannot fully appreciate the joy of fulfillment unless you have traveled through the eye of adversity, been seriously defeated by

setbacks, or had the crushing wave of disappointment knock you down so that you considered not getting up again.

"Nearly every person that has ever succeeded has experienced setbacks. Perhaps they witnessed their dreams shattered, their aspirations scorned and ridiculed, or their goals dashed against the bricks of financial institutions. They have had to deal with frustration, rejection, and disappointment and learn ways to rebound from their setbacks.

"There will be times as you travel your path that you encounter obstacles. As you make your way there is always the potential that you will fail... the challenge in those moments is to tap your source of determination so you can pick yourself up, dust off the grit of embracement, wounded pride or shaking confidence, and move forward, you will need to take time to process the experience, so that you may heal properly, and so you gain perspective and learn from what happened.

"If you are going to succeed in life and consequently be fulfilled, then you must face the disappointments and failures that life deals you, and discover the value inherent in them. The wise ones however are the ones who do and who use those setbacks as opportunities to grow so that they may venture forward toward future success."

In the same context of reassessment, let's review and summarize what steps and tools we have covered in the book so far.

Please go ahead and pick your one, two or three meaningful steps and tools that you found to be as extremely beneficial for your success and journey.

MILESTONES

Step
5

SELF
AWARENESS

Step
6

CHALLENGING

Step
7

PERSISTENCE

Step
8

CRISIS
MANAGEMENT Step 9

REASSESSMENT Step 10

SELF
CONTROL Step 11

SUCCESS Step 12

ULTRA
GOAL

Step
I

LONG/MID/SHORT
TERM GOALS

Step
I

S.M.A.R.T GOAL

Step
I

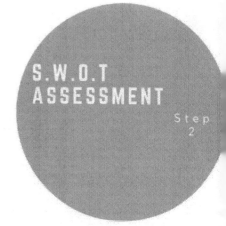

S.W.O.T
ASSESSMENT

Step
2

REALISTIC/IDEAL
/STRETCHED
GOALS
Step
3

GOALS
RESETTING
Step
3

ACTION PLAN
Step
4

CONTINGENCY
PLAN
Step
4

MICRO GOALS

Step 5

SUPER POWER

Step 6

U MODEL &
PEAK
PERFORMANCE

Step 7

ENERGETIC
COPING
TECHNIQUES Step 8
* HEADS UP
* BREATHING
* SMALL STEPS
* SLOW DOWN

PSYCHOLOGICAL
COPING TECHNIQUES
* MILESTONES
* POSITIVE
REINFORCEMENT
* INNER DIALOGUE
* VISUALIZATION

Step 9

CHANGES'
FLEXIBILITY

Step 10

VISUALIZATION

Step 11

SETTING
A NEW
GOAL

Step 12

STATUS
CONTROL
TASK

Step 10 – Task

1. Re-assess your situation according to your plan and goals.

2. Explain what steps and skills you chose and why are they helpful for you.

YOUR
EXERCISES
FLEXIBILITY

Step 10 – Status Control: Flexibility Exercise

Reassessing the situation is essential when trying to achieve a long-term goal, as changes often occur during the path to success, and we need to be able to adapt and adjust.

We must develop and practice flexibility in the face of changes when the reality does not suit the plan, or when the possibility of achieving the original goal is low. Creative thinking is part of the process of problem solving when we need to come up with a new goal, strategy, or plan.

❖ Therefore, I have provided you the fitness section of my flexibility exercises. This is similar to the earlier section on stretching, but will make you even more flexible!

❖ **Disclaimer**: Consult with your physician or other health care professional before starting this or any other fitness program to determine if it is right for your needs. Do not start this fitness program if your physician or health care provider advises against it. If you experience faintness, dizziness, pain or shortness of breath at any time while exercising you should stop immediately.

SEATED EASY SIDE BEND

Set/Time: hold pose for 15-30 seconds (each side)

1. Sit down and gently lean over toward your left side, and press your left palm and forearm into the ground alongside your body.

2. Extend your right arm straight up overhead. Stay here for at least 15 seconds of stretching.

SEATED WITH CROSSED LEG

Set/Time: hold pose for 15-30 seconds (each side)

1. Sit and hold your right knee next to your chest. Hold the leg with your arms crossed for support. Keep your back straight.

2. Keeping your abs tight, exhale as you hold in the pose with your leg bent and tight to your upper body.

SEATED ONE LEG FORWARD BEND

Set/Time: hold pose for 15-30 seconds (each side)

1. Sit up tall. Extend your right leg forward and flex your right foot. Bend your left foot in toward your inner thigh. Exhale and fold your torso over your right leg.

2. Try to reach the line of your toes with your hands. Inhale and exhale as you extend the stretch of the right leg, trying to reach far out with your hands and your head to the front knee.

RUNNER'S STRETCH

Set/Time: hold pose for 15-30 seconds (each side)

1. Come into a kneeling position with your knees directly under your hips. Slowly lower your back to the ground.

2. Take your right foot forward and bend it with the foot against the surface. Relax your arms across your hips and breathe deeply into the position.

SEATED WIDE LEG STRADDLE

Set/Time: hold pose for 15-30 seconds

1. Sit up tall and open your legs to the sides until you feel a moderate tension.

2. Walk your hands forward between your legs so you feel a little tension (but not so much that it is uncomfortable).

SPLIT

Set/Time: hold pose for 15-30 seconds (each side)

1. Come into a low lunge with your right leg straight forward. Gently lower your legs to the surface.

2. Rest your hips on the ground. Your hips and shoulders should be working toward facing the front.

*This exercise is advanced, and an easier variation would be to bend the right knee instead, resting in front of you in a reverse V.

RECLINING SINGLE KNEE HUG

Set/Time: hold pose for 15-30 seconds (each side)

1. Lie down on your back. Hug your left knee gently into your chest. With each exhale, draw your knee closer to your right shoulder.

2. Close your eyes, and relax. Stay here for up to half a minute, deep breaths.

Set/Time: hold pose for 15-30 seconds

1. Kneel on the ground and walk your hands forward until they are slightly past your chest line. Straighten your arms, keeping your torso long and strong, and look directly ahead at the floor. Your knees can be hip width apart.
2. Exhale and slowly lift your upper body a bit more, extending your back.

STEP 11 – SELF-CONTROL

"There is nothing either good or bad, but thinking makes it so."

-William Shakespeare

In many cases, peak events or achieving the desired success is far harder to handle than failure. Often, there is a popular fear of success, which can lead to performance anxiety that yields poor performance as a manifestation of self-sabotage.

As we saw in Step 5, big goals carry risks – at least, that is how our subconscious mind is likely to perceive them – because success means change and uncertainty more than failure does. Since we tend to fear the unknown, certain questions might arise when facing the possibility of success. For example in sports, what will happen in the competition? Will I succeed in my goal? Will I win? What if I don't make it to the finish line?

Self-sabotage is an unconscious, automatic mental reaction, meant to remove threats of impending changes. Many times, we do not even recognize that this fear is present. Success exposes us to new and unfamiliar situations, though, which may make us uncomfortable and stressed. This new situation will test our limits and enhances our responsibility.

Self-sabotaging is partially about generating excuses. For example, we may blame illness, bad luck, and more, but for the most part, these excuses lead us to actively work against ourselves by doing the opposite of what we truly want to do in order to succeed.

In Step 9, we discussed coping techniques to manage stress or setbacks. These tools can be just as useful in regaining some self-control, especially visualization, guided imagery, and breathing exercises.

As part of the mental preparation training in Step 10 – Self-Control, I recommend my mentees to think about their big day or peak event when they finally achieve their goal. I ask them to imagine what will happen at that day and how they will perform and succeed. In business, I ask my entrepreneurs to write down their future winning speech as if they have already succeeded in their goal, and to keep the letter in an envelope that they will open when the time comes.

In physical training, I help my mentees with guided imagery and meditation session. Here is an example of a guided session:

"Lay down on your back in a comfortable spot, in a pleasant environment. Close your eyes and relax your muscles. Try to loosen each muscle, especially the tense ones throughout your body. Relax your arms, hands, fingers... legs, feet, toes, forehead, lips and eyes... take a big breath – inhale... Exhale. Again. Inhale... Exhale... Listen to your breathing, feel your lungs fill with air, and then exhale.

"Imagine the day of the competition. Imagine yourself coming to the event. There is a lot of excitement, there are many runners walking to the starting line. You are standing on the starting line, ready to achieve the goal you have been training to accomplish. Finally, the race starts. You are happy and feeling energized and refreshed. After a few minutes, you are getting warmed up and start to pass and overtake some of the other runners.

"Time passes. You have been running for a while and you are starting to feel your legs are tensed-up and a bit tired, you feel your calves and thighs. You keep moving forward, head up. You feel your heart pumping, you are sweating, you breathe deeply. You have reached the halfway mark and there is another half of the race to overcome. You calculate the remaining distance in your mind and focus on the closest target, repeatedly. You imagine the finish line, how you cross it and how soon it is all going to be over. You remind yourself how hard you have worked to come this far. You are getting closer to the finish line, increasing your pace, you are about to finish the race and you are the happiest that you have ever remembered yourself being!

"You see your family at the finish line, cheering for you, and you know that no matter where you finish – you are already a winner. You receive your medal for completing the race, you cool down, you hydrate yourself and look back at the race to remind yourself what you have just overcome and achieved.

"Take a big breath – Inhale... Exhale... Again. Inhale... Exhale... Listen to your breathing, feel your lungs filled with air, and then emptied. Before you wake up from this visualization exercise, take the good memories of this experience with you and think about them while trying to accomplish the goals you have set!"

SELF- CONTROL
TASK

Step 11 – Task

1. visualize and write down your winning speech as if you have already achieved your goal and success.

STEP 11 – SELF- CONTROL: WALL RESISTANCE EXERCISES

You are one step away from achieving your goal. All the hard work you have put in is finally coming to an end, and your real test and peak event is right around the corner!

This step forces you to practice self-control so that you do not get cold feet or quit at the most important moment. Easing stress is an important action and skill that we will use when we deal with big tasks that are valuable for us.

❖ Therefore, I have provided you the fitness section of my boxing and wall-resistance exercises, so you can unpack the energy, noises, and weights you have been carrying on your back, as well as practice deep breathing techniques in a few of the following exercises.

❖ **Disclaimer**: Consult with your physician or other health care professional before starting this or any other fitness program to determine if it is right for your needs. Do not start this fitness program if your physician or health care provider advises against it. If you experience faintness, dizziness, pain or shortness of breath at any time while exercising you should stop immediately.

STANDING PUSH KICK

Set/Time: 10-15 repetitions (each side)

1. Stand close to a punch pole. Raise your knee high up and in a fast movement conduct a side kick while fully extending the leg to hit the pole.

2. Simultaneously give a punch with your hands, as if you are about to defend your head. Press the front foot deeper onto the pole.

SIDE KICK

Set/Time: 10-15 repetitions (each side)

1. Stand close to a punching pole that's at your back. In a quick movement, lift up your knee close to your chest and immediately extend your leg backward to a side kick, while turning your face to the pole.
2. Simultaneously extend your opposite hand to a straight punch. Hold in the posture for a moment, and then conduct the exercise again from its starting position.

FIRST STRIKE

Set/Time: 20-30 repetitions (each side)

1. Stand close to a punching pole with one foot forward. Hold your right arm close to your chest with a fist.

2. Exhale as you strike a straight punch with our other fist, looking at the target. Rotate the working hand in each repetition.

HANDSTAND

Set/Time: hold pose for 5-10 seconds

1. Stand close to a wall that's at your back. Bring both hands to the floor under your shoulders. Straighten your arms.
2. Lift your legs one after the other and support them against the wall. Breathe and hold in posture once you find your balance.

BACK ARCH STRETCH

Set/Time: hold pose for 5-10 seconds

1. Stand close to a wall or pole that's at your back. Lift your hands high up and slowly while breathing deeply, arch your back while trying to touch, and hold the wall or pole with your palms.

2. Straighten your look toward the pole and make sure you do not over-stretch your back.

SQUAT IN AIR

Set/Time: hold pose for 5-15 seconds

1. Sit facing a wall. Bring your hips high up while your body weight is supported by your arms.
2. Press your feet against the pole with knees at a straight angle. Exhale as you tighten your abs and hold in the position for a few moments.

ARMS STAND

Set/Time: hold pose for 10 seconds

1. Sit next to a wall, placing it at your back. Put your arms and palms on the floor and slowly lift your legs one by one so that they are climbing the wall.
2. Keep one leg slightly bent against the wall supporting your weight, and extend your other leg, so that it is in a line with your arms.

WALL PUSH-UP

Set/Time: hold pose for 10-20 seconds

1. Lie next to a wall with your stomach on the floor.

2. Slowly lift your upper body with your palms climbing on the wall while bending your knees. Keep your palms in line with your chest, and inhale as you hold the posture.

STEP 12 – SUCCESS

"When the way comes to an end, Then change – Having changed, you pass through."

-I Ching

You have come this far in the course, and you have gone through the twelve steps to success of the Ultra Leadership Method. I hope that you have gained several new physical and psychological tools and skills which will benefit you in your personal and professional life. These can be applied to any goal or purpose that you want to achieve, as long as it is measurable and manageable.

Setting goals and making sure they are the right goals, building a plan and making sure it is the right plan, checking and re-testing your abilities and condition, being challenged, being consistent, learning self-control and overcoming difficulties and crises are the core values and characteristics necessary to becoming a winner!

You will be pleasantly surprised to see how what you have learned in this book can also be applied to other areas of your life. This book contains the most important skills that I have learned from running five ultramarathons and from more than eight years of training and coaching people to improve their running, leadership, and management skills.

Let me conclude this book with a quote about dealing with success and its implications, from Cherie Carter's book, *If Success is the Game, These are the Rules*:

"One of the biggest challenges to succeeding is maintaining your perspective. Before you reached your new level of success, you were familiar with the view. You knew the landscape and were all acquainted with the terrain. Then the game board shifted, and nothing looks familiar anymore. The view changed and the terrain may feel foreign under your feet. Everything seems different. It is easy to get swept up in the excitement and seduced by the glamour and feel of victory. The true test of what you are made of comes when you realize the goals you have been striving toward all along. Can you enjoy your success without letting it distort your vision? Can you embrace your new level of success without it inflating your ego? Can you stay aligned with your values when new temptations beckon? The greater your success is, the more challenging the test. At a certain level of playing the success game, you will likely encounter four significant lessons: maintaining integrity, arrogance, greed and power. The more you achieve, the harder it is to resist seduction by the dark side of success. Your greatest challenge will be to stay grounded in yourself as you scale the heights of greatness."

SUCCESS
TASK

Pick your new goal, and start a new journey!

If you have thoughts, comments, or ideas about this book, please write to me at the following email address:

Ash@ultraleadershipmethod.com

You are also invited to visit my website and to subscribe to my newsletter:

https://ultra.training

BIBLIOGRAPHY

Bailey, R. (2006). Physical education and sport in schools: A review of benefits and outcomes. Journal of School Health, 76(8), 397-401.

Bashan, Hadas, Ashmoret Rishona, Menta magazine, Israel. Issues, October 2014, October 2015.

Battista, J., & Almond, R. (1973). The development of meaning in life. Psychiatry, 36(4), 409-427.

Baumeister, R. F. (1991). Meanings of life. Guilford Press. A division of Guilford Publication, Inc.

Buehler, Roger; Dale Griffin; Michael Ross (1994). Exploring the "planning fallacy": Why people underestimate their task completion times. Journal of Personality and Social Psychology. American Psychological Association. 67 (3): 366–381.

Burton, D., & Vidic, Z. (2010). The roadmap: Examining the impact of a systematic goal-setting program for collegiate women's tennis players. TSP, 4,427-447.

Canfield, Jack; Switzer, Janet (2015). The success principles - 10th anniversary edition: How to get from where you are to where you want to be. Amazon.com.

William Morrow Paperbacks. Retrieved 21 December 2015.

Carter-Scott, Ph.D., Chérie (2000). If success is a game, these are the rules. New York: Broadway Books. ISBN 0-7679-0426-5.

Caspersen, C. J., Powell, K. E., & Christenson, G. M. (1985). Physical activity, exercise, and physical fitness: Definitions and distinctions for health-related research. Public Health Reports, 100(2), 126-131.

Covey, Stephen R. The 7 habits of highly effective people: Restoring the character ethic. New York: Free Press, 2004. Print.

Deiner, E., Oishi, S., & Lucas, R. E. (2003). Personality, culture, and subjective well-being: Emotional and cognitive evaluations of life. Annual Review of Psychology, 54, 403-425.

Duckworth, A. L., Peterson, C., Matthews, M. D., & Kelly, D. R. (2007). Grit: perseverance and passion for long-term goals. *Journal of personality and social psychology*, *92*(6), 1087.

Drucker, P., The practice of management, Harper, New York, 1954; Heinemann, London, 1955; revised edn, Butterworth-Heinemann, 2007.

Frankl, V. E. (1963). Man's search for meaning: Revised and updated. WW Publisher.

Gore, J. S., & Cross, S. E. (2006). Pursuing goals for us: Relationally autonomous reasons in long-term goal pursuit. Journal of Personality and Social Psychology, 90(5), 848.

Grant, A. (2013). *Give and take: A revolutionary approach to success*. Hachette UK.

Greenleaf, C., Boyer, E. M., & Petrie, T. A. (2009). High school sport participation and subsequent psychological well-being and physical activity: The mediating influences of body image, physical competence, and instrumentality. Sex Roles, 61(9-10), 714-726.

Hackman, J.R. and C.G. Morris, 1975. Group tasks, group interaction process, and group performance effectiveness: A review and proposed integration, in: L. Berkowitz. ed., (Academic Press, New York, NY). 45-99.

Humphrey, Albert (December 2005). SWOT analysis for management consulting. SRI Alumni Newsletter. SRI International.

Imai, Masaaki. Kaizen: The key to Japan's competitive success. New York, itd: McGraw-Hill (1986).

Kruglanski, A. W.; Mayseless, O. (1990). Classic and current social comparison research: Expanding the perspective. Psychological Bulletin. 108 (2): 195–208.

Lee, Felissa K.; Sheldon, Kennon M.; Turban, Daniel B.; Personality and the goal-striving process: The influence of achievement goal patterns, goal level, and mental focus on performance and enjoyment, Journal of Applied Psychology. 88(2): 256–265. doi:10.1037/0021-9010.88.2.256. PMID 12731709.

Matthews, Gail. (2007). Goals research. Dominican University, CA.

McCormack, Mark, What they don't teach you at Harvard Business School: Notes from a street-smart executive, New York: Bantam, (1984).

McGarty, Craig (Ed); Yzerbyt, Vincent Y. (Ed); Spears, Russell (Ed). (2002). Stereotypes as explanations: The formation of meaningful beliefs about social groups (pp. 1-15). New York, NY, US: Cambridge University Press, x, 231 pp. http://dx.doi.org/10.1017/CBO9780511489877.002

Mishal, Ashmoret, Ashmoret Mishal's column, Shvoong article, Israel, Jan.-Dec.2016.

Mishal, Ashmoret, Ashmoret Mishal's column, The best One Online magazine, Jan.-Dec.2016.

Morgeson, Frederick P.; DeRue, D. Scott; Karam, Elizabeth P.; Leadership in teams: A functional approach to understanding leadership structures and processes. Journal of Management, Vol 36(1), Jan 2010, 5-39.

Penedo, F. J., & Dahn, J. R. (2005). Exercise and well-being: A review of mental and physical health benefits associated with physical activity. Current Opinion in Psychiatry, 18(2), 189-193.

Robbins, Tony, Unlimited power: The new science of personal advancement. Magill Book Reviews. January 1990.

Sagiv, L., & Schwartz, S. H. (2000). Value priorities and subjective well-being: Direct relations and congruity effects. European Journal of Social Psychology, 30(2), 177-198.

Sheldon, K. M., & Elliot, A. J. (1998). Not all personal goals are personal: Comparing autonomous and controlled reasons for goals as predictors of effort and attainment. Personality and Social Psychology, 24(5), 546.

Sheldon, K. M., & Elliot, A. J. (1999). Goal striving, need satisfaction and longitudinal well-being: the self-concordance model. Journal of Personality and Social Psychology, 76(3), 482.

Shepherd, D., Ryan, C., & Schofield, G. (2012). Psychological well-being, self-reported physical activity levels, and attitudes to physical activity in a sample of New Zealand adolescent females. Psychology, 3(6), 447-453.

Turkay, S. (2014). Setting goals: Who, why, how?. Manuscript.

Warburton, D. E., Nicol, C. W., & Bredin, S. S. (2006). Health benefits of physical activity: The evidence. Canadian Medical Association Journal, 174(6), 801-809.

Wicker, P., & Frick, B. (2015).

White, Alasdair (1 December 2009). From comfort zone to performance management: Understanding development and performance. White & MacLean Publishing.

Wooten, L. P., & James, E. H. (2008). Linking crisis management and leadership competencies: The role of human resources development. Advances in Developing Human Resources, 10(3), 352-379.

Yukl, G. A., & Mahsud, R. (2010). Why flexible and adaptive leadership is essential. Consulting Psychology Journal: Practice and Research, 62, 81–93.

ABOUT THE AUTHOR

Ashmoret Mishal is the youngest Israeli ultramarathon runner female champion (125 miles) and the founder of the "Ultra Leadership Method" and 12 Steps to Success. This program is being taught around the world to help in leading people to success using endurance sports and the ultramarathon mind techniques for accomplishing long term goals.

Made in the USA
Columbia, SC
12 February 2018